FREE AUDIO EXAMPLES
Available for Streaming
or Download –
No Signup
Required!

HOW TO F
GUITAR IN

Daily Lessons for
Absolute Beginners

By Troy Nelson

ISBN: 9798523623035   Copyright © 2021 Troy Nelson Music LLC
International Copyright Secured. All Rights Reserved.

HOW TO GET THE AUDIO

The audio files for this book are available for free as downloads or streaming on *troynelsonmusic.com*.

We are available to help you with your audio downloads and any other questions you may have. Simply email *help@troynelsonmusic.com*.

See below for the recommended ways to listen to the audio:

Download Audio Files (Zipped)	Stream Audio Files
• Download Audio Files (Zipped)	• Recommended for CELL PHONES & TABLETS
• Recommended for COMPUTERS on WiFi	• Bookmark this page
• A ZIP file will automatically download to the default "downloads" folder on your computer	• Simply tap the PLAY button on the track you want to listen to
• Recommended: download to a desktop/laptop computer *first*, then transfer to a tablet or cell phone	• Files also available for streaming or download at *soundcloud.com/troynelsonbooks*
• Phones & tablets may need an "unzipping" app such as iZip, Unrar or Winzip	
• Download on WiFi for faster download speeds	

To download the companion audio files for this book, visit: troynelsonmusic.com/audio-downloads/

INTRODUCTION

Acoustic or electric? That's the first question every aspiring guitarist must answer. For beginners, each instrument has its merits and drawbacks. But, really, you can't go wrong with either one. I always tell new students to pick the instrument they see themselves playing most often in the future. If you decide down the road that you want to switch to the other—or just want to become equally proficient on both—you can always apply to your new guitar what you've learned on your primary instrument. Although they have a different look and sound, acoustic and electric guitars are fundamentally the same instrument, containing the same notes, in the same places.

The fact that you purchased this book means you've probably put some thought into the acoustic versus electric debate. And you've made a great choice! The acoustic guitar is a diverse instrument that has a place in just about every music genre and application. And perhaps the best part—and why it's such a popular guitar choice—is that no amplifier is necessary to be heard in small-to-medium-sized venues. And, for gigging guitarists, it means no lugging around a 50-pound (or more) amp!

While everything in this book will translate to electric guitar, the topics we will be covering have been chosen specifically because of their importance to the *acoustic* guitar. Although both instruments are fundamentally the same, some guitar techniques are especially important to the acoustic guitar because of the tonal and technical differences between the two instruments.

Before you dive into the lesson portion of the book, let's preview the topics that you'll be practicing each day.

CHORDS
Music consists of three main components: melody, harmony (chords), and rhythm. Therefore, equipping yourself with different chord qualities (major, minor, etc.) and chord types (open chords, barre chords, etc.) is imperative. Each day, we'll spend 15 minutes learning some of the most important chords for acoustic guitar, starting with basic open chords and working our way up to four-, five-, and six-string barre chords. By the end of the two-week program, you'll have an arsenal of guitar chords at your disposal!

CHORD PROGRESSION
When two or more chords are strung together, a *chord progression* is created. In this section, the chords that you learned in the previous section will be applied to a common chord progression. This section is also dedicated to learning an important guitar technique: strumming. Each day, just as new progressions are introduced, so too are new rhythms and strumming patterns.

ARPEGGIOS

An *arpeggio* is the notes of a chord played one at a time. In this section, we'll work on arpeggiating the chords that you've been practicing in the previous two sections. Arpeggios are a popular harmonic and melodic devise in music and sound particularly good on acoustic guitar due the instrument's resonant hollow body.

FINGERPICKING

While the exercises in the first three sections are meant to be performed with a pick, this section is entirely devoted to fingerpicking. The sound of bare fingers on the strings of an acoustic guitar is hard to beat and therefore worthy of a deep dive. Here, we'll revisit the arpeggios from the previous section but toss the pick and, instead, play them "fingerstyle."

TECHNIQUE

Each day, a new acoustic guitar technique will be introduced in this section. While all the techniques featured in this section are transferable to electric guitar, we'll be going over ways certain techniques are commonly applied to acoustic, everything from hammer-ons, pull-offs, and slides to double stops, hybrid picking, and percussive thumb slaps.

MELODY/SCALES

This section is devoted to getting your right-hand picking chops in order. Single-note picking takes considerable time to develop—and is something you'll continue to work on throughout your guitar-playing career—so working on it daily is imperative. We'll spend most of the first week flatpicking, or "picking," familiar melodies. On Day 6, however, we'll turn or attention to scales, learning a new scale each day for the remainder of the book. Consequently, as you work on your picking technique, you'll be simultaneously learning new melodies and scales.

WEEK 1 AND WEEK 2 REVIEWS

Days 7 and 14 are review days. Here, we'll spend the entire 90 minutes of the lesson on practicing a short song. On Day 7, we'll work on "When the Saints Go Marching in," and on Day 14 we'll practice "Battle Hymn of the Republic." Each song is presented two ways: as a strumming arrangement and as a fingerpicking arrangement. These arrangements feature chords, strum patterns, and arpeggios that have been practiced the previous six days. The melody is also included in the strumming arrangement so you can continue to work on your alternate picking.

HOW TO USE THIS BOOK

Granted, 90 minutes of practice per day can seem daunting—and that's OK! Just because the book is structured to teach you acoustic guitar in 14 days doesn't mean you have to follow the program precisely. On the contrary, if you have, say, 30 minutes to devote to the book each day, then simply extend each lesson (day) to a three-day practice session. The material is there for you to use, whether you get through the book in 14 days or 40.

While the 14-day plan is the goal, it's probably unrealistic for some. The important thing is to stick with it, because the material in this book will have you playing acoustic guitar fluently and confidently. How quickly just depends on the amount of time you're able to devote to getting there.

Before you begin your daily sessions, however, I suggest spending 10–15 minutes listening to the accompanying audio to get a feel for the forthcoming exercises, as well as reading through each section's introductory material to better understand what you're about to learn. That way, you can spend the *full* 90 minutes (or however much time you have to practice that day) playing the music examples.

To help keep you on track in your practice sessions, time codes are included throughout the book. Simply set the timer on your smart phone to 90 minutes (1:30) and move on to the new section every 15 minutes. Or, you can set the timer to 15 minutes (0:15) and move on to the next lesson when the timer goes off, repeating this step for every section.

Next, set your metronome (or drum loop, click track, etc.) to a tempo at which you can play the exercise all the way through without making too many mistakes (40–50 beats per minute is probably a good starting point for most exercises). Once you're able to play the exercise cleanly, increase your tempo by 3–4 BPM. Again, make sure you can play through the exercise without making too many mistakes. If the speed is too fast, back off a bit until your execution is precise. Continue to increase your tempo incrementally until it's time to move on to the next section.

There will be times when the timer goes off and you feel like you didn't adequately learn the material. When this happens, I suggest moving on to the next section, nonetheless. It may seem counterintuitive, but it's better to continue progressing through the book than to extend the practice time in order to perfect the material. After you've completed the book, you can always go back and review the exercises. In fact, I recommend going through the book a second—or even third—time. Making steady progress, while not always perfectly, keeps you mentally sharp and motived. Focusing too much on any one exercise is a sure way to sidetrack your sessions.

Lastly—and this is important—if you ever feel yourself getting physically fatigued or pain develops in any part of your body, especially your hands or arms, immediately take a break until the discomfort subsides, whether it's for 10 minutes, an hour, or for the rest of the day. You never want to push yourself beyond your physical limits and cause permanent damage. As mentioned earlier, the material isn't going anywhere; you can always go back to it when you're feeling 100%.

PARTS OF THE GUITAR

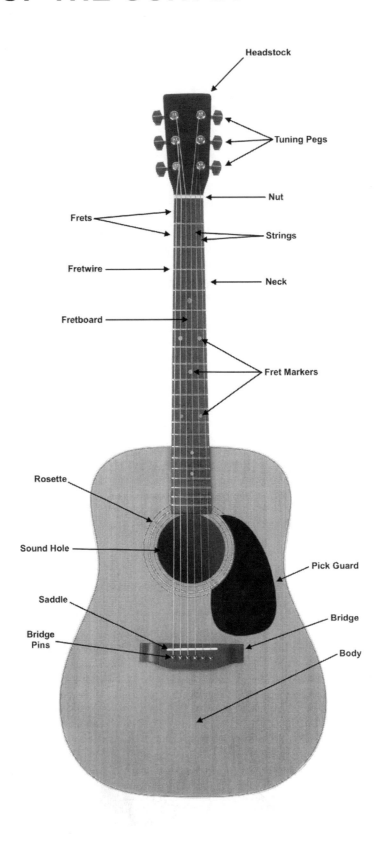

Headstock

Tuning Pegs

Nut

Frets

Strings

Fretwire

Neck

Fretboard

Fret Markers

Rosette

Sound Hole

Pick Guard

Saddle

Bridge

Bridge Pins

Body

TUNING METHODS

In standard tuning, the strings of the guitar are tuned as follows: **E–A–D–G–B–E** (low to high). It's called "standard" tuning because it's far and away the most commonly used guitar tuning. Let's look at a few ways you can go about tuning your instrument.

TUNING APPS

For beginners, the easiest way to tune the guitar is to download a free guitar-tuner app to your smart phone. Most work well but let the star ratings help you decide.

Once you have the tuner app downloaded to your phone, simply pluck each string individually while adjusting its corresponding tuning peg until you reach the desired pitch. The tuner will indicate whether the string is above (sharp) or below (flat) the desired pitch. Loosening the string lowers the pitch, and tightening the string raises the pitch.

Start with string 6, the low E string (standard tuning contains *two* E strings), which is the thickest of the six strings (and closest to the ceiling). While adjusting the tension, pay strict attention to the slack in the string. If it becomes too loose or too taut, you'll need to turn the tuning peg in the opposite direction. Let the tuner be your guide, but the string's tension (or lack thereof) will also let you know if you're heading in the right direction. After you get the low E string to pitch, work your way through strings 5–1 in the same manner. Newer strings tend to go out of tune more frequently than worn strings, so you'll need to tune up more frequently if your guitar has a fresh set.

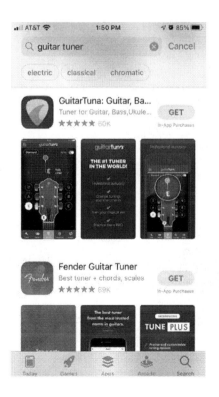

ELECTRONIC TUNERS

Although electronic tuners have seen their popularity decline since the advent of tuning apps, they're still favored by many guitarists. Electronic tuners come in all shapes, sizes, and colors. Some of the most popular are of the clip-on variety, which fasten to your guitar's headstock. Unlike app tuners, which identify pitch via a built-in mic, clip-on tuners like the popular Snark brand (see below) pick up each string's pitch via vibrations from the headstock. The popularity of these tuners is due to accessibility and accuracy, as well as not having to use an instrument cable. Since clip-on tuners use vibration detection, environmental noise doesn't interfere with the tuning process, resulting in stable, precise tuning experiences. And some clip-on tuners even come with an external mic, allowing for sound-detection tuning, as well.

Another option is the multi-purpose electronic tuner, which includes several tuning modes (chromatic, guitar, ukulele, etc.), as well as a metronome. These tuners contain an instrument-cable input so you can connect your electric or acoustic-electric guitar for accurate tuning in loud environments. These tuners tend to be a little pricier than the clip-on models, but their multi-function capabilities might be appealing to you.

THE KEYBOARD METHOD

If you have a piano (or keyboard) handy, you can always tune your guitar's strings to the piano's corresponding keys.

Take a look at the diagram below. If you move 12 white keys to the left of middle C, you'll find the key that corresponds to the pitch of the low E string (string 6). Simultaneously pluck the string and sound the piano key until both pitches sound the same (i.e., in tune). The piano's sustain pedal will come in handy here. From E, move up three white keys to find the key that matches the pitch of string 5, A. Sound both notes until the pitches match. Use the diagram to find the pitches for the remaining four strings: D, G, B, and E.

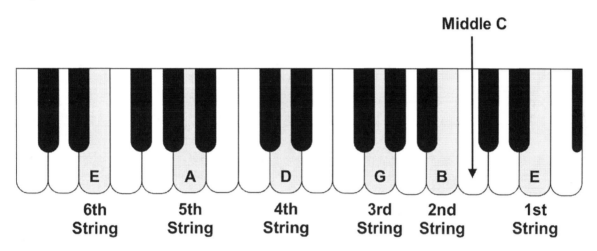

RELATIVE TUNING

Sometimes you'll find yourself stuck without a tuning source. Don't fret—you can use a method known as *relative tuning*. As long as your low E string is in tune—or at least close to its proper pitch—you can tune the other five strings so that the strings are in tune relative to one another.

Follow these steps:
1. Adjust your 6th (low E) string until you think it's in tune (for this purpose, close is good enough)
2. Fret the note at fret 5 of string 6, A, which is the same pitch as the open 5th string. Pluck this fretted note while also sounding the open 5th string. Adjust the pitch of string 5 until the two notes match.
3. Fret the note at fret 5 of string 5, D, which is the same pitch as the open 4th string. Pluck these two notes simultaneously, adjusting the pitch of string 4 until the two notes match.
4. Fret the note at fret 5 of string 4, G, which is the same pitch as the open 3rd string. Pluck these two notes simultaneously, adjusting the pitch of string 3 until the two notes match.

5. Fret the note at fret 4 of string 3, B, which is the same pitch as the open 2nd string. Pluck these two notes simultaneously, adjusting the pitch of string 2 until the two notes match.

6. Fret the note at fret 5 of string 2, E, which is the same pitch as the open 1st string. Pluck these two notes simultaneously, adjusting the pitch of string 1 until the two notes match.

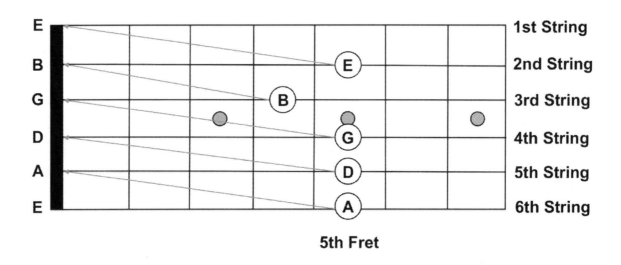

5th Fret

TUNING TO THE AUDIO

Now that you're acquainted with the aforementioned tuning methods, here's an easy one: download the tuning notes that accompany this book (all audio files are downloadable and can be found at *troynelsonmusic.com* or our SoundCloud page, *soundcloud.com/troynelsonbooks*). As you listen to each note, adjust the corresponding tuning peg until the string matches the recorded pitch. Once you've adjusted all six strings, your instrument should be in standard tuning: E–A–D–G–B–E (low to high).

◀)) TUNING NOTES: E–A–D–G–B–E

PROPER POSTURE

You can play the guitar two ways: sitting or standing. Neither approach is better than the other, and often context will determine which you use. For example, if you're playing in a band setting, then you'll most likely choose to stand (you might look rather silly sitting while your singer and bassist are standing). When you're in your bedroom practicing, you may choose to sit, especially if it's a long session. That said, standing while practicing is also a good habit to get into. In fact, some guitarists will mimic their upcoming gigs by playing through their entire set list while standing.

SITTING

If you choose to sit, be sure to position yourself at the edge of your seat, with a relaxed posture. Set the guitar on the leg that's on the same side as your picking hand; for example, if you'll be strumming and picking the strings with your right hand, then set the guitar on your right leg. Conversely, if you'll be picking and strumming with your left hand, then place the guitar on your left leg. The guitar should rest on your thigh, near your torso, with the neck resting parallel to the floor.

STANDING

If you choose to stand, you will need a guitar strap, which fastens to strap buttons located on the upper bout and base of the guitar's body. Adjust the strap so that the guitar is positioned at the lower part of your torso, where your arms feel relaxed but not rigid. If you feel like you're having to reach too much with your arms to grip the neck and strum the strings, then you'll likely need to raise the strap a bit. On the flip side, if you feel tension in your neck, shoulders, or arms, then you will need to loosen your strap. Strive for comfort.

PICKING & STRUMMING

Although fingerpicking will be covered throughout the book, the pick-hand technique we will focus on predominantly is flatpicking. *Flatpicking*, also known simply as "picking," involves plucking the strings with a flat, tear-shaped guitar pick. Most guitar picks are made from plastic or plastic-like materials and come in many sizes, colors, and thicknesses.

Choosing a pick that is best for you will take some time and is largely dependent on what style of music you play. If you find yourself mostly strumming folk songs, then a thin pick might be best because they tend to create a warmer sound than thick picks. Conversely, if you plan to play a lot of single-note lines (i.e., solos), then you might prefer a thicker pick. Experiment with as many types as you can; eventually, you'll find one that speaks to you.

Hold the pick between the thumb and index finger of your pick hand. The more pick surface you leave exposed, the less control you will have over the pick. This approach is popular for strumming because it results in a warmer tone (and strumming requires less precision).

If you plan to do a lot of single-note picking, you'll likely want to leave less pick surface exposed, gripping the pick near its tip. This gives you more control of the pick, resulting in more efficient upstrokes and downstrokes. In fact, in addition to gripping the pick near its tip, many guitarists will slant the pick semi-perpendicular to the strings to create less friction and, in turn, more speed.

As mentioned in the introduction, fingerpicking, or "fingerstyle," is a popular picking method for acoustic players because of its warm tone and versatility. Generally, in fingerstyle playing, the thumb is assigned to the bass strings (strings 4–6), and the index, middle, and ring fingers are assigned to strings 3, 2, and 1, respectively (the pinky is used infrequently). In other words, the thumb typically handles multiple strings while the other three fingers are assigned to specific strings—although these assignments can change to accommodate new chords and melodies. In music notation, the pick-hand fingers are labeled as follows:

Thumb: *p* (*pulgar*)
Index: *i* (*indice*)
Middle: *m* (*medio*)
Ring: *a* (*anular*)
Pinky: *c* (*chiquito*)

CHORD DIAGRAMS & TAB

The music examples in this book are presented in a couple of different formats: chord diagrams and rhythm tab. In this section, we're going to go over each format so you'll be able to quickly apply the music to your instrument as you go through the book. Let's start with chord diagrams.

CHORD DIAGRAMS

A *chord diagram*, or *chord frame*, is simply a graphical representation of a small section (usually four or five frets) of the guitar neck, or fretboard. Vertical lines represent the guitar's six strings, horizontal lines represent frets, and black dots indicate where your fingers should be placed. Although a bit counterintuitive, chord diagrams are presented as though you're looking at the neck while the guitar is held vertically in front of you rather than from a more natural horizontal position. Nevertheless, chord frames are a good way to quickly understand how a chord should be "voiced," or fingered.

A thick, black horizontal line at the top of the diagram indicates the guitar's nut (the plastic-like string-spacer at the end of the fretboard). When this is present, the chord typically incorporates one or more open strings, which are represented by hollow circles above the frame. Conversely, when an open string is not to be played, an "X" will appear above the frame.

When more than one note is fretted by the same finger, or "barred," a slur encompasses the notes. *Barre chords* get their name from this technique, which can range from two to six strings. If a chord is played higher up the neck, above the 4th of 5th fret, the nut is replaced by a thin horizontal line and the fret number is indicated next to the lowest fret (highest in the diagram). Sometimes—but not always—the chord's fingering is included at the bottom of the frame: 1 = index, 2 = middle, 3 = ring, 4 = pinky, and T = thumb.

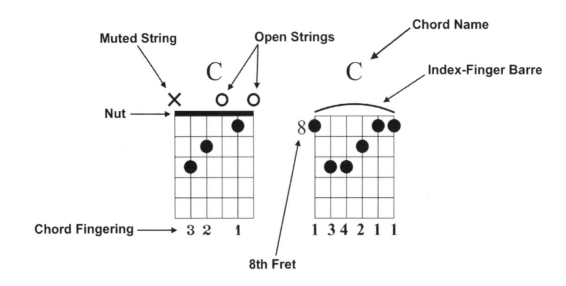

TAB

As a form of music notation, tab has been around for centuries. However, it has really exploded in popularity among guitar players the past few decades, particularly since the advent of the Internet. The reason for its popularity is the simple fact that it's so easy to learn and use.

A tab staff looks much like a standard treble or bass clef; however, if you look a little closer, you'll notice that it contains *six* lines instead of five. Those six lines represent the six strings of the guitar, with the low E string positioned at the bottom, and the high E string at the top. Tab contains no key signature because there are no notes to deal with; instead, numbers are placed on the strings to represent the frets of the guitar neck. So, for example, if you see the number 3 on the 6th (low E) string, you would fret that string at fret 3. Or, if you see the number 0 stacked on the 3rd and 4th strings, you would strum those strings together, open (unfretted).

Sometimes you'll see tab accompanied by standard notation, and other times you'll see tab-only music (we'll be using the latter in this book). Tab-only music often includes rhythm symbols (stems, flags, beams, rests, etc.), as well. Rhythm symbols in tab are the same as those you'll find in standard notation but the noteheads are replaced by fret numbers. Because we incorporate rhythm, the tab includes a time signature and requires a fundamental understanding of rhythm, which we'll cover extensively throughout the book (unlike standard notation, we won't have to worry about key signatures, however).

The time signature is a pair of numbers that are stacked on top of each other and displayed at the beginning of a piece of music (immediately after the key signature in standard notation). The top number indicates how many beats comprise each *measure*, or *bar* (the space between the vertical *bar lines*), while the bottom number indicates which note is equivalent to one beat (2 = half note, 4 = quarter note, 8 = eighth note, etc.). For example, in 4/4 ("four-four") time, each measure contains four beats (upper number), and quarter notes are equivalent to one beat (bottom number).

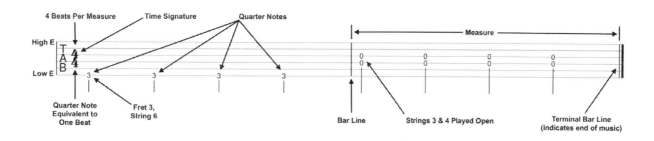

17

WEEK 1: OPEN CHORDS

In our first week of lessons, we'll be covering all the topics mentioned in the book's introduction (chords, progressions, arpeggios, fingerpicking, technique, and melody) but with an emphasis on *open chords*, or chords that contain one or more open strings. Open chords are some of the easiest chords to play on guitar, so they're a good place to start. Next week, we'll focus on a more challenging type of chord, barre chords. Let's get started.

DAY 1

CHORDS: C & Am (1:30–1:15) 🔊

Our first two chords, C and Am, belong to the same "chord family" (key of C major) and are fingered, or "voiced," similarly. In our first exercise, the C chord is voiced with the ring (string 5), middle (string 4), and index (string 2) fingers, with strings 1 and 3 played "open." You'll need to drop your fret-hand wrist a little to get enough arch on your fretting fingers to allow the open strings to ring true.

Strum the chords in whole notes, counting "1, 2, 3, 4" for each one. In other words, strum downward through strings 5–1, allowing your metronome to click four times before strumming again. Listen to the audio track to hear how this exercise should sound.

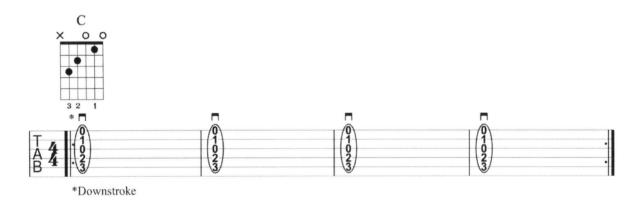

*Downstroke

To voice the Am chord, simply reposition your ring finger, moving it from fret 3, string 5 to fret 2, string 3. The other two fingers, middle and index, will remain in place from the C chord. You'll notice in the chord diagram that string 5 is now played open, so you'll still be strumming through the same five strings. Like our previous exercise, this example is played exclusively in whole notes. Remember to count: "1, 2, 3, 4," etc.

18

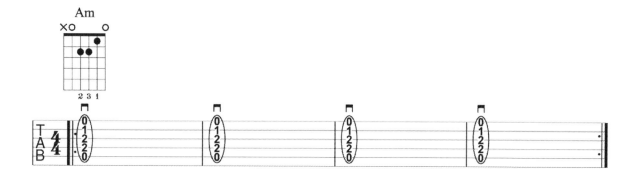

CHORD PROGRESSION: Am–C (1:15–1:00) 🔊

Now we're going to take the chords we just learned and create a simple two-chord progression: Am–C. The examples below are similar to our previous exercises, only now we'll be switching between the two chords.

The first exercise involves strumming the Am chord twice (wholes notes), followed by two strums of the C chord. Since the chords share similar voicings, you can keep your index and middle fingers in place throughout, shifting your ring finger from string 5 (C chord) to string 3 (Am), and back.

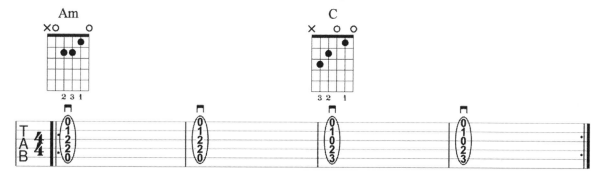

Our second exercise is very similar to the first, only now the chords change twice as fast, or *every* measure. If the metronome gets distracting, just practice this exercise without it, focusing more on the chord changes themselves than on making them in time.

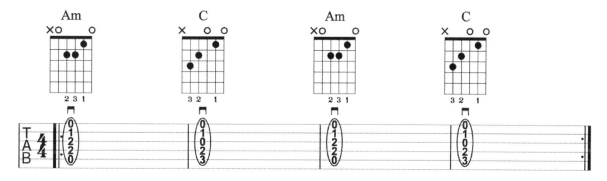

ARPEGGIOS (1:00–0:45) 🔊

In this section, we're going to continue our Am and C chord studies by arpeggiating each one (an *arpeggio* is simply the notes of a chord played one at a time). In the exercise below, the Am–C progression from the previous section is performed with an ascending arpeggio pattern. Instead of strumming through the chords, use your pick to pluck each string of the chord (downstrokes are used throughout, as indicated above the staff), one after the other, allowing the strings to clearly ring out.

The rhythm used here incorporates both quarter notes and whole notes. In 4/4 ("four-four") time—the time signature used here—quarter notes receive one beat, so you'll be plucking a new string on each beat, or click of the metronome. In measures 2 and 4, however, you'll hold out the last note of the chord (the open high-E string) for the measure's full duration, or a whole note. You can use these whole notes strategically: as they ring out, start shifting your ring finger to its position for the next chord.

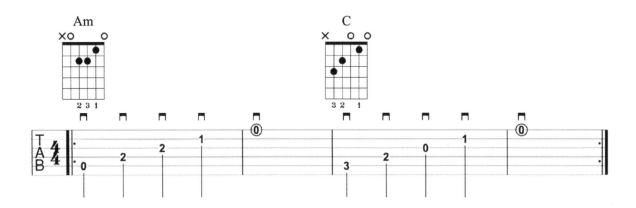

FINGERPICKING (0:45–0:30) 🔊

Now we're going to perform the arpeggio exercise that we just worked very similarly, only instead of plucking each string with the pick, we're going to use our pick-hand fingers exclusively. In the exercise on the next page, the plucking fingers are indicated above the staff. As you can see, the thumb will pluck string 5 *and* string 4, while the index, middle, and ring fingers will pluck strings 3, 2, and 1, respectively. Since the picking is consistent for both chords, you can place much of your focus on making the changes with your fret hand.

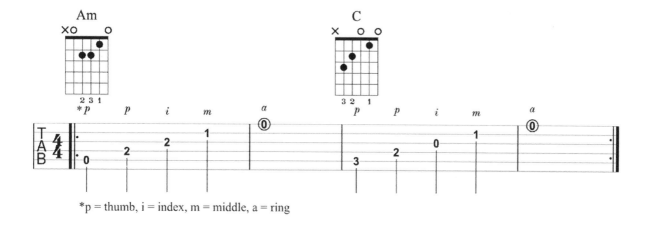

*p = thumb, i = index, m = middle, a = ring

TECHNIQUE: HAMMER-ON (0:30–0:15) 🔊

A *hammer-on* is a technique that involves articulating a note with a fret-hand finger rather than with the pick (or pick-hand finger). In notation and tab, hammer-ons are notated with a slur. For example, in the exercise below, the note at fret 1, string 2 is sounded by "hammering" the index finger onto the fretboard from the open string.

This example is very similar to the arpeggio exercises from the previous two sections, only here we'll initially voice the Am and C chords without the index finger in place. Instead, we'll pluck string 2 open and then hammer the index finger onto the fretboard to sound the note at fret 1. Notice that no picking is involved to sound the second note— it's articulated entirely by the action of the hammer-on.

The rhythms used in this example are similar to the ones used in the previous two sections; however, instead of whole notes in measures 2 and 4, we now have a quarter note (the "hammered" note) and a *dotted* half note, which receives *three* beats. So, the quarter note falls on beat 1, and the dotted half note occupies the remaining three beats (2, 3 and 4). Listen to the audio to hear the hammer-ons and rhythms in action.

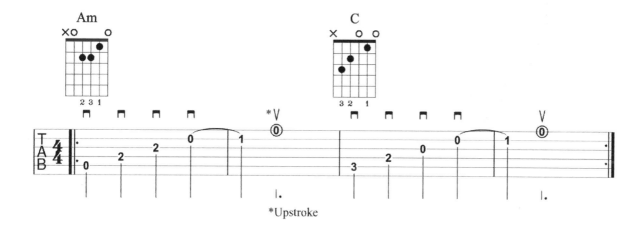

*Upstroke

21

MELODY: JINGLE BELLS (0:15–0:00) 🔊

In our final section of the day, we're going to focus on our picking hand, using a familiar melody, "Jingle Bells," to practice alternate picking, a technique that involves continuously alternating downstrokes and upstrokes. The four-bar excerpt below is played entirely on strings 1–2. Start with a downstroke and then alternate your picking strokes throughout the passage (follow the directions above the staff). After you've played through the melody a few times, try starting with an upstroke. As for your fretting hand, use a combination of your index (fret 1) and ring (fret 3) finger to voice the fretted pitches.

Rhythmically, most of the example is performed in a quarter- and half-note rhythm. A *half note*, as you may have guessed, receives two beats in 4/4 time. One exception occurs on beats 3–4 of measure 3, where a *dotted* quarter note and an eighth note are played. A *dot* increases the duration of the note by half of its original value; therefore, the duration of a dotted quarter note is one-and-a-half beats (1 + 1/2 = 1 1/2). (If you recall, a dotted *half* note receives three beats. That's because the half note gets two beats and the dot adds half of that, or one beat: 2 + 1 = 3.)

The eighth note, meanwhile, possesses half the rhythmic value of a quarter note, so it receives half a beat—or one eighth the value of a whole note. A full measure of eighth notes is counted as follows: "1-and, 2-and, 3-and, 4-and," etc. Use the audio track and the counting prompt below the staff to help with the rhythm.

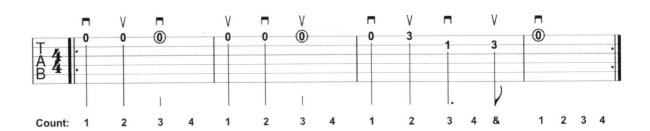

CHORDS: G & Em (1:30–1:15) 🔊

Today, we're going to learn two new chords and a new rhythm. Like C and Am, G and Em belong to the same chord family (G major); unlike last week's chords, however, these two do not share similar voicings. Therefore, you might need to put in a little extra work to get them under your fingers.

In our first exercise, the G chord is played in a steady half-note rhythm. In 4/4 time, a half note receives two beats, or half the equivalence of half a measure. Therefore, you'll need to strum on beat 1 *and* beat 3 of each measure—twice as often as a whole note. Set your metronome to a slow tempo (40–50 BPM), gradually increasing your speed as you get more and more comfortable. If you struggle to get the open strings to ring out clearly, drop your fret-hand wrist down a bit to give your fingers a little more arch.

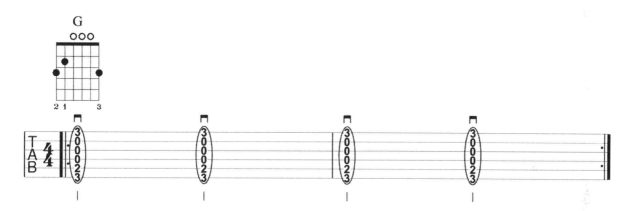

The Em chord is somewhat similar to the Am chord, only the middle and ring fingers are voiced one string pair lower, and the index finger is not included. Again, if you have trouble getting the open strings to ring out clearly, drop the wrist of your fretting hand down a bit. This will enable you to voice the notes of the chord with your fingertips.

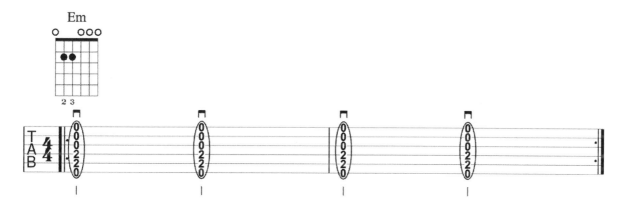

CHORD PROGRESSION: G–Em–C–G (1:15–1:00)

Today's progression, G–Em–C–G, incorporates three of the four chords we've learned so far. Our first exercise is played in strict half notes, with chords changing at the top of each measure. Go slowly and use a downward strum for each chord attack.

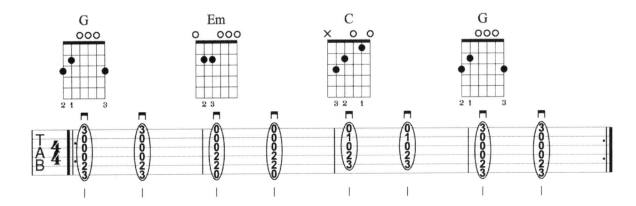

Now let's speed up the changes. In the exercise below, the chords change on beat 3 of each measure—or twice as fast as our previous exercise. Practice this example several times without a metronome, focusing on making the changes cleanly. Then add in the metronome, set to a slow tempo, and try to make the changes in time. Don't get discouraged if you struggle; instead, just keep working at it!

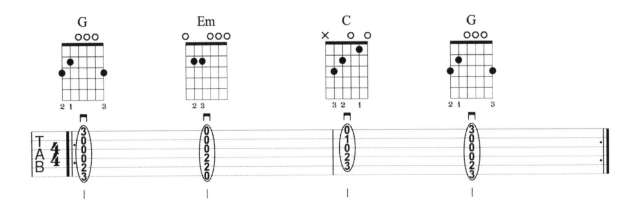

ARPEGGIOS (1:00–0:45) 🔊

Now let's try arpeggiating the chords of our new G–Em–C–G progression. In the exercise below, each chord of the progression is ascended and descend over the course of two measures. Use continuous downstrokes as you ascend the chords, and continuous upstrokes as you descend, allowing each note to ring out. Notice that the G and Em arpeggios skip over string 5 on the way up the strings. This is a common occurrence when arpeggiating chords on guitar, so it's never too early to start getting used to skipping strings.

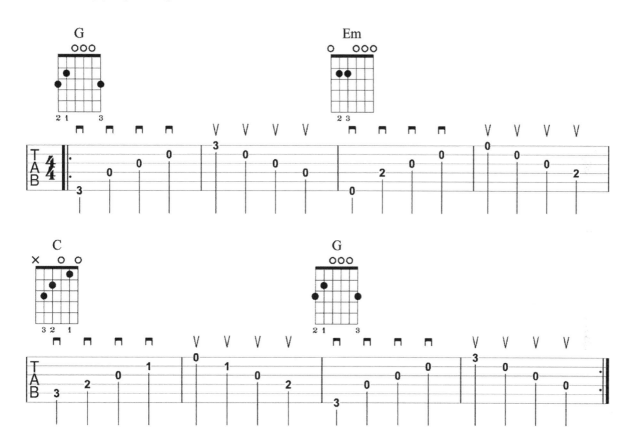

FINGERPICKING (0:45–0:30) 🔊

Now we're going to fingerpick the arpeggios from the previous section. Like yesterday's fingerpicking exercise, the index, middle, and ring fingers of your picking hand will handle the notes on strings 3, 2, and 1, respectively, with the thumb handling the lower three strings. This means that the thumb will play back-to-back notes for each chord, including having to skip over string 5 for the G and Em chords.

Since the thumb's job is much more involved than the other three fingers, you might want to spend some extra time on it. For example, you could isolate the two notes assigned to the thumb, playing them back to back, over and over in a loop. Once the movement feels somewhat natural, you can add in the other three fingers, playing the arpeggios as written.

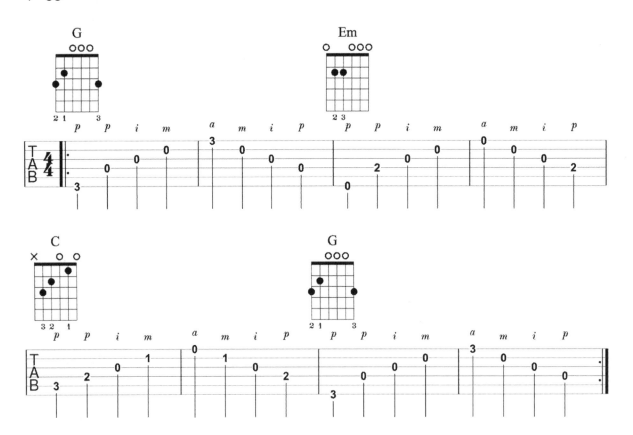

TECHNIQUE: PULL-OFF (0:30–0:15) 🔊

A *pull-off* is essentially the opposite technique of a hammer-on. Instead of hammering onto the fretboard to sound a note, a pull-off involves "pulling" a finger from a fretted pitch to sound a lowered fretted note or open string. In other words, the first note is plucked and the second note is sounded by the action of the fret-hand finger—the pull-off.

The exercise below is a combination of yesterday's hammer-on exercise and the arpeggio exercises that we've been working on today, only here we'll be executing pull-offs on string 2 instead of hammer-ons. To perform the pull-offs, pluck the fretted note (fret 1) and, as you lift your index finger from the fretboard, pull the string downward every-so-slightly, essentially using the fretting finger to pluck the string. Fortunately, since we're playing Am and C chords, the only shifting that needs to happen in the fret hand is with the ringer finger; the other fingers can stay in place.

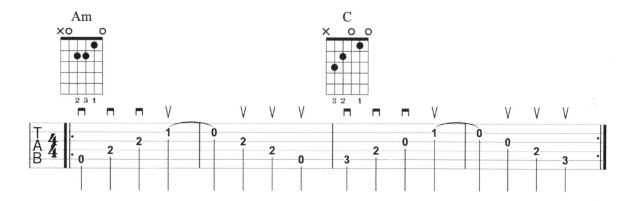

MELODY: AMERICA THE BEAUTIFUL (0:15–0:00) 🔊

Now we're going to use a four-bar excerpt from "America the Beautiful" to work on our alternate picking. Use alternate (down-up) picking throughout (see picking directions above the staff). For the fret hand, use your index, middle, and ring fingers to voice the notes at frets 1, 2, and 3, respectively. Also, notice that this melody shares a lot of the same rhythms—quarter notes, dotted quarter notes, and eighth notes—as yesterday's melody, "Jingle Bells."

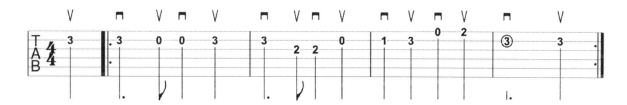

DAY 3

CHORDS: F & Dm (1:30–1:15) 🔊

Although the F chord contains no open strings and therefore technically isn't an "open chord," it gets lumped in with the other open chords, nonetheless. The reason is because, when a guitarist is strumming open chords and the song contains and F chord, this is the closest and best option.

The "open" F chord is based on a first-fret, six-string barre chord shape, but instead of incorporating all six strings, it's often limited to four strings, reducing the number of barred strings from six to just two. Still, for beginner guitarist, the two-string barre is challenging, therefore I've included three options below. The first exercise features a simpler three-string version that leaves out the top string. Play through the exercise and see how it feels.

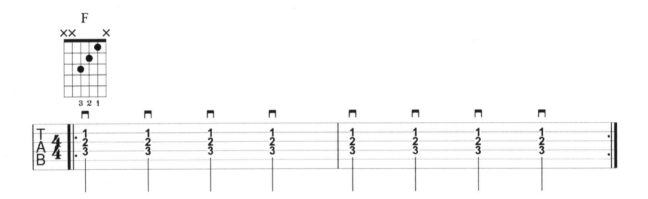

Another option is the open Fmaj7 (F major 7th) chord shown below. The open high-E string gives the chord a different sound but, since it's still major in quality, it functions like a standard F major chord. And, since it contains an open string, it's technically an open chord. Play the example below a few times to hear how it sounds. And be sure to let the open string ring!

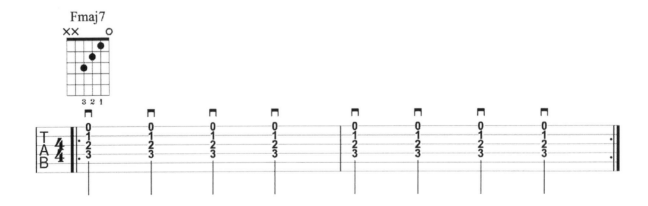

Our third option is the most common way beginners are taught to play the F chord. It's tricky, however, because you need to use the index finger to barre the top two strings at fret 1. Play through the exercise a few times to test drive the voicing, then feel free to use whichever version of the F chord is easiest for you at this time. Eventually, you'll want to be able to play each of them fluently.

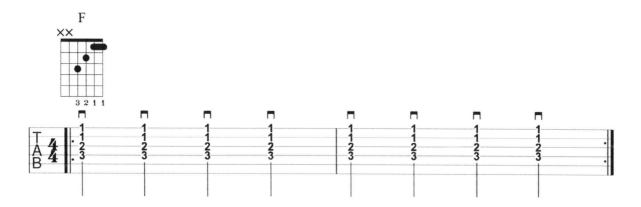

Now let's finish off this section with another member of the F chord family, Dm. This chord *does* contain an open string (string 4) and is voiced somewhat like the F chord. For example, the index finger will hand the note on fret 1, string 1, and the middle finger voices the note at fret 2, string 3. However, now the ring finger is relocated to fret 3, string 2, enabling string 4 to ring open. Play the exercise a few times and then move on to the next section.

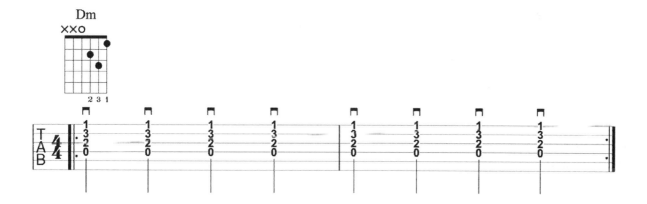

CHORD PROGRESSION: Dm–F–C–G (1:15–1:00)

Now let's take our two new chords, Dm and F, and combine them with a couple of chords we've learned the previous two days, C and G, to create a four-chord progression: Dm–F–C–G. In the first example below, each chord is strummed in quarter notes for a full measure. In exercise 2, the chords change every two beats.

Here's a tip for the Dm–F change: When you voice the Dm chord, use your index finger to barre across strings 1–2. Even though you'll be playing string 2, fret 3 with the ring finger (making the barre unnecessary), by having the two-string barre in place, you'll only need to shift your ring finger to make the F chord change. This makes the transition much more efficient, and a lot of guitar playing is about finger efficiency.

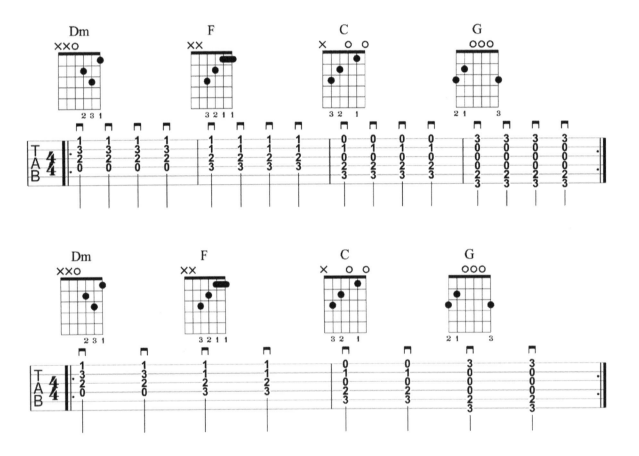

30

ARPEGGIOS (1:00–0:45) 🔊

Now we're going to use our Dm–F–C–G progression to practice a new arpeggio pattern. In the exercise below, the lowest note of each chord is played on the downbeat (beat 1 of the measure) with a downstroke. This is followed by three straight upstrokes that arpeggiate the three highest notes of the chord. Let the notes ring out as you pluck them. If you struggle to make the chord changes in time, practice the example several times without a metronome, adding it in once you feel comfortable with the voicings.

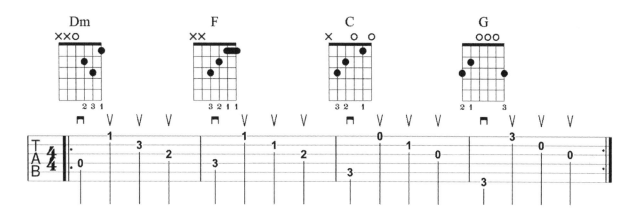

FINGERPICKING (0:45–0:30) 🔊

As we've done the previous two days, now we're going to play the arpeggio exercise from the previous section, fingerstyle. Instead of downstrokes with the pick, here we're going to pluck the lowest note of each chord with our thumb. This is followed by an *a–m–i* (ring–middle–index) pattern on strings 1–3, respectively.

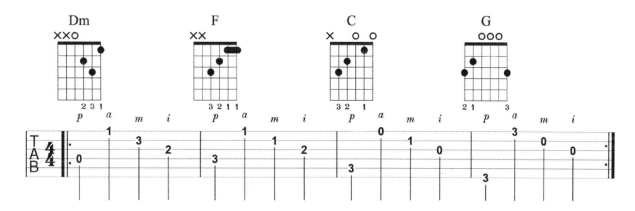

TECHNIQUE: SHIFT SLIDE (0:30–0:15) 🔊

The technique we'll be working on today is the *shift slide*, which involves picking a fretted note, sliding the fretting finger up or down the fretboard to a lower or higher pitch, and then plucking the string a second time. To practice this technique, we're going to alternate shift slides with chords from our Dm–F–C–G progression.

In the exercise below, use your index finger to voice the note on fret 3, string 1, then pluck the string with a downstroke, shift your index finger down two frets, and re-pluck the string with an upstroke. This is immediately followed by a strum of the Dm chord. Follow this same sequence for the F and C chords, as well. For the G chord, however, we're going to perform a pull-off in lieu of the shift slide. Again, if you struggle to play this exercise in time, turn off the metronome until you feel like you have a good grasp on performing the slides and chords in tandem.

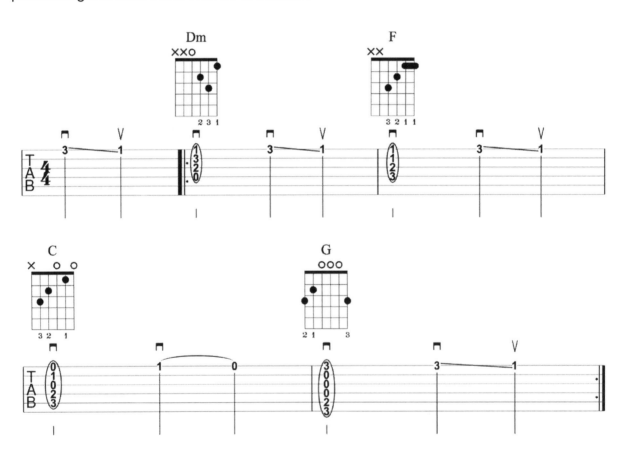

MELODY: ANCHORS AWEIGH (0:15–0:00)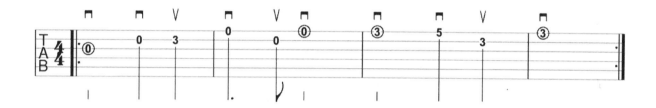

Today, we're going to use a four-bar excerpt from "Anchors Aweigh" to further refine our picking skills. Follow the picking directions indicated above the staff, but also feel free to experiment with your own. With this type of melody, where the rhythms vary (much like our previous two picking exercises), there are no hard-and-fast rules with respect to picking. For example, instead of using back-to-back downstrokes in measures 1 and 3, you could instead choose to alternate pick the entire melody: down-up-down-up-down-up, etc.

As for the fretting hand, use your index finger for the notes at fret 3, and your ring finger for the note at fret 5. When moving from the last note of measure 3 to the final note of the melody, simply roll your index finger downward instead of lifting your finger from the fretboard and reapplying it. In other words, use the index finger as a small, two-string barre.

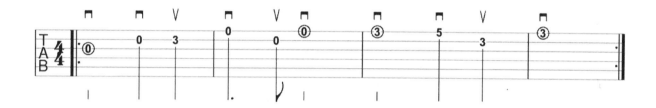

DAY 4

CHORDS: A & D (1:30–1:15) 🔊

Today, we're going to turn our attention to the chords A and D. Let's start with A. Like yesterday's F chord, when played in open position, the A chord can be voiced a few different ways. As a beginner, I suggest playing through each of the first three examples below to determine which voicing you like best and go with that one—at least for now. Eventually, you'll be able to voice all three chords with equal ease and let the musical context determine which one you use.

The first example is probably the most common way to finger the open A chord. It involves fretting strings 4–2 at fret 2 with the index, middle, and ring fingers, respectively. This voicing can feel a little cramped, which is one reason why some guitarists prefer to use an alternate voicing, such as the ones below.

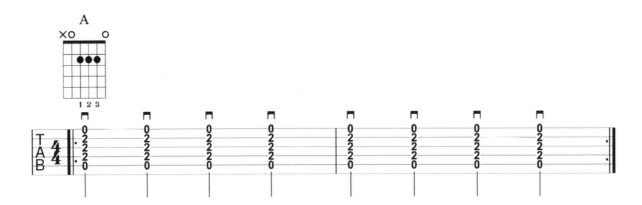

Because of the cramped nature of our first A chord, some guitarists prefer to use the voicing below. It's similar to the previous one, only the index and middle fingers are flip-flopped. This mitigates the cramped, tight nature of the previous voicing. Try this one out and see how it feels.

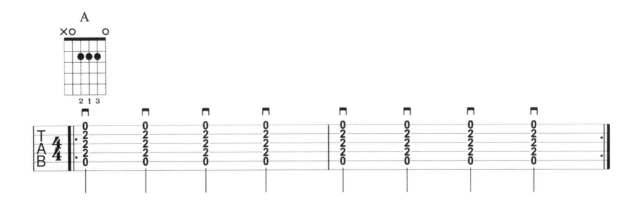

The third version of the A chord is actually a *barre* chord. Instead of using the first three fingers of our fretting hand, we'll barre the notes on strings 4–2 with just our index finger. Because of this approach, the open high-E string is omitted, giving this chord a slightly different sound. Personally, when I'm playing acoustic guitar, I like the sound of the ringing open string, so I usually play version 1; however, the chord below is my go-to voicing when I'm playing electric guitar, particularly with a distorted tone.

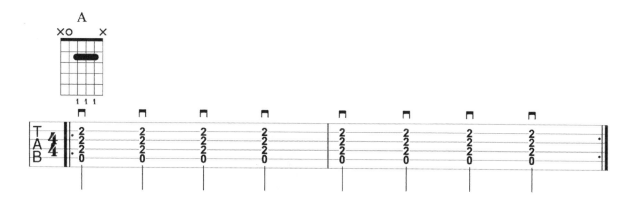

The open D chord is typically played just one way, as shown below. This voicing involves fretting the notes on fret 2 with the index (string 3) and middle (string 1) fingers, and the note on fret 3 (string 2) with the ring finger. Be sure to drop the wrist of your fretting hand down so you can voice all three notes with the tips of your fingers (your fret-hand thumb should be on the back of the neck, near the middle); that way, you can get all the strings to ring out clearly.

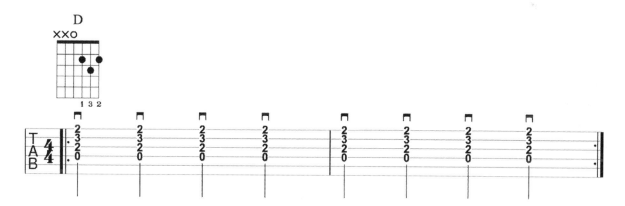

CHORD PROGRESSION: D–G–Em–A (1:15–1:00) 🔊

Today's progression, D–G–Em–A, is a collection of chords that we've learned throughout the first four days. Rhythmically, the exercises alternate quarter notes and eighth notes. Count these as follows: "1, 2-and, 3, 4-and," etc.

In the first exercise, the chords change every measure; in exercise 2, the chords change every two beats. Take these slow at first and be sure to follow the strumming directions: down, down-up, down, down-up, etc. Spend about 7–8 minutes on each and then move on to the next section.

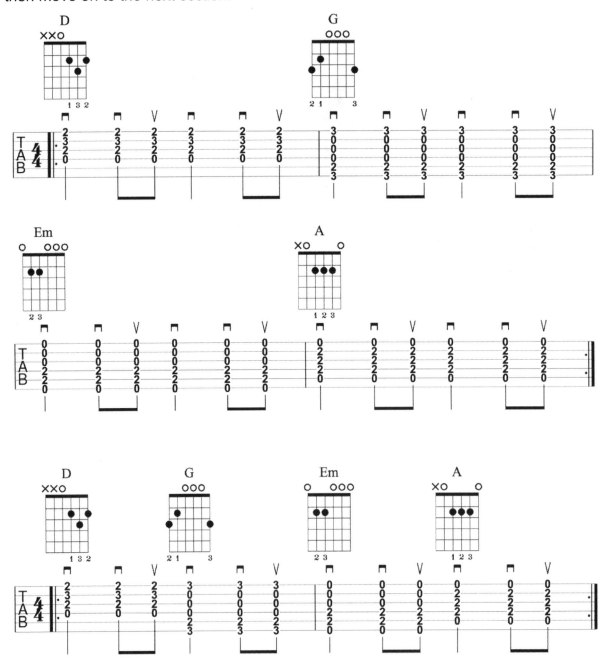

ARPEGGIOS (1:00–0:45) 🔊

Now we're going take the progression from the previous section and arpeggiate the chords, one measure each. The pattern used here involves picking the lowest note of each chord (the root) with a downstroke and then using back-to-back upstrokes to articulate the highest two notes of the voicing. This two-beat pattern is repeated on beats 3–4, only the note on beat 3 is plucked on string 3. Listen to the audio track to hear these arpeggios in action.

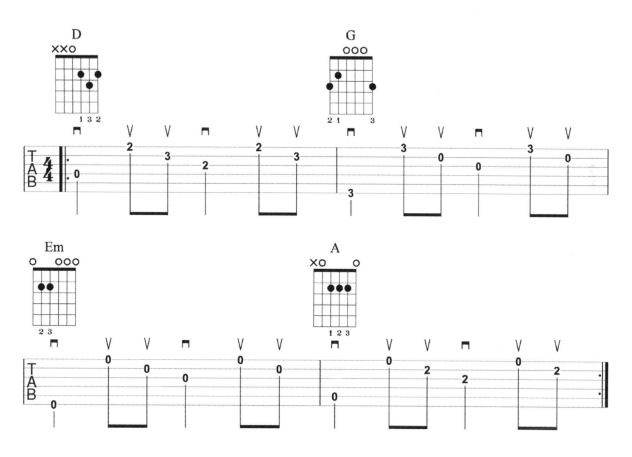

FINGERPICKING (0:45–0:30) 🔊

Now let's take the exercise that we just worked on in the Arpeggios section and fingerpick each note. Here, we're going to use an *a–m–i–a–m* (ring–middle–index–ring–middle) finger pattern for the notes on strings 1–3, with the thumb handing the root notes on beat 1. Before you attempt to play the entire exercise, practice each chord in isolation to get comfortable with the pick-hand fingering. Then string together the four chords and play through the exercise a few times before moving on.

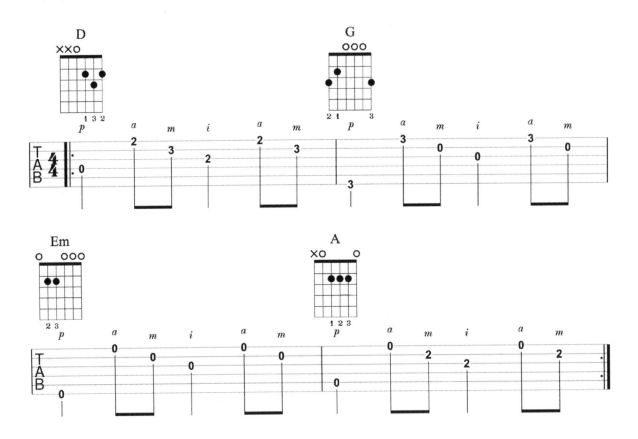

TECHNIQUE: LEGATO SLIDE (0:30–0:15) 🔊

A *legato slide* differs from a shift slide in that only the first note is picked. In other words, the first note is plucked and then the fretting hand moves to a higher or lower pitch, which is sounded via the slide rather than by the pick or pick-hand finger.

In the example below, legato slides are used to create a short, two-note *motif* (repetitive melodic idea) on string 3 to offset the chord changes—the same D–G–Em–A progression that we've been working on throughout today's lesson. Remember, pick the first note and then slide to the second note without re-picking the string. Be sure to follow the pick/strum directions indicated above the staff.

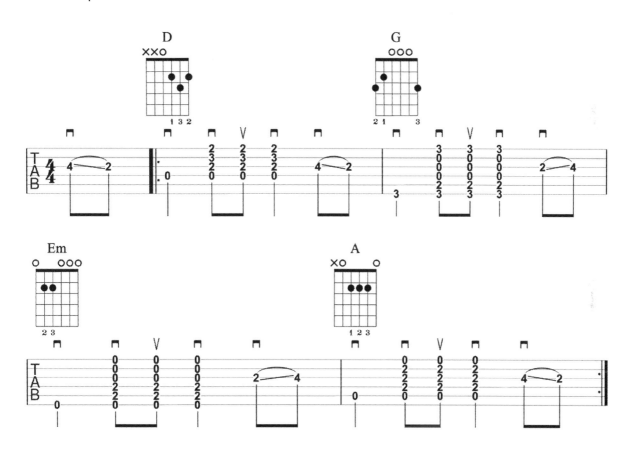

MELODY: AULD LANG SYNE (0:15–0:00) 🔊

We're going to add a new string to our picking exercises: string 4. This four-bar excerpt from the New Year's anthem "Auld Lang Syne" starts with a pickup note, which is plucked on string 4 (and beat 4). This is followed in measure 1 by another note on string 4, only this time fretted at fret 4.

The picking directions provided here are only suggestions, as this passage can be picked a number of different ways. Experiment and try coming up with your own picking sequence. Just be sure to alternate your picking strokes as much as possible, as this will come in handy when playing at faster tempos.

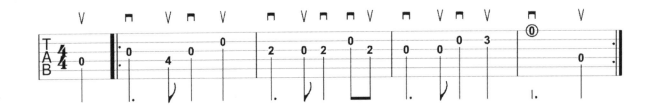

DAY 5

CHORDS: E, E7 & A7 (1:30–1:15) 🔊

Today's chord studies focus on the one open-position major chord that we have yet to practice, E, as well as a new chord type, the dominant 7th—specifically, E7 and A7. The chords we've learned so far are basic three-note major and minor chords, or *triads* (notes are often doubled in triad voicings), whereas *7th chords* contain *four* notes and have both major and minor properties, giving them a "bluesy" sound.

Our first chord, E, is fairly straightforward; just be sure to arch your fingers enough to allow the top two strings to ring out clearly.

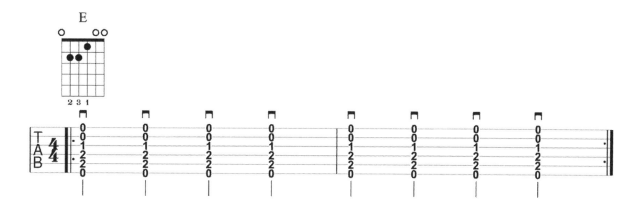

If you have a handle on the E chord, E7 shouldn't give you too much trouble. To voice the E7 chord, simply apply your fret-hand fingers to the fretboard like you would if you were playing the E chord, but instead of adding your ring finger to string 4, let that string ring open (unfretted). That's it!

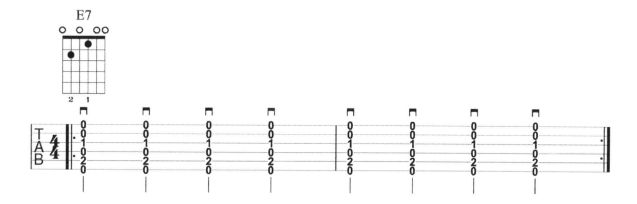

Like E7, the A7 chord is very similar to it its major counterpart—in this case, A. In the exercise below, string 3 is allowed to ring open, rather than voiced at fret 2. This is how the "regular" A chord becomes A7. While the voicing below suggests using your middle and ring fingers for the fretted pitches, feel free to experiment with an index-ring combo—in other words, similar to version 1 of the A chord that we learned yesterday, only without fretting string 3. You could even play it with a combination of your index and middle fingers. Use whichever works best for you.

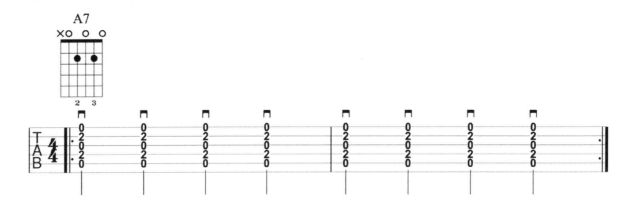

CHORD PROGRESSION: A7–D–E7–A7 (1:15–1:00) 🔊

Now we're going to take our new A7 and E7 chords, add the D chord from yesterday, and create a bluesy-sounding A7–D–E7–A7 progression. In addition to the new chords, the big takeaway from this exercise is the rhythm, which features unyielding eighth notes—an important strum pattern to know and master. It may seem pretty simple, but strumming a string of eighth notes like this—in time—is very challenging, so be sure to practice along to a metronome, hitting each click with a downstroke and filling the spaces in between with an upstroke.

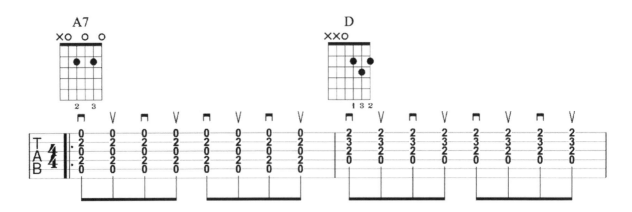

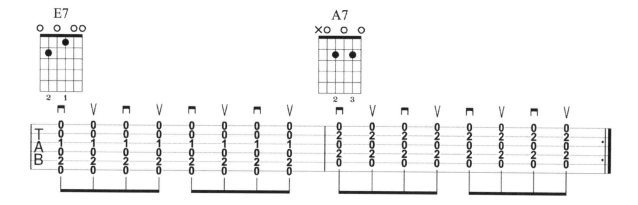

One trick that will help you with this type of strum pattern is to implement cheat strums. A *cheat strum* involves strumming open strings—in place of an actual chord—on the strum that immediately precedes the next chord change. For example, in the exercise below, instead of holding the A7 chord through all four strums in measure 1, you would remove your fretting hand from the fretboard and strum open strings (top 3 or 4) in place of the chord itself. This approach helps you get your fret hand in place for the next chord—in this case, D. And, because it happens so quickly at moderate-to-fast tempos, the listener never notices the difference. You can use cheat strums to facilitate all the chord changes in this example.

This exercise features the same chord progression as the first example, only here the chords change twice as fast. Again, use strictly alternate (down-up) strumming throughout.

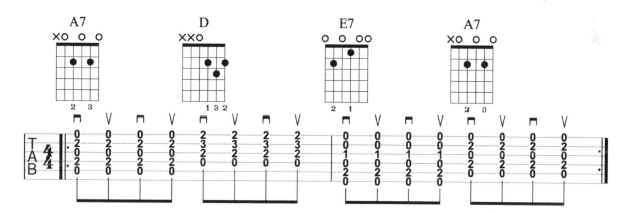

ARPEGGIOS (1:00–0:45) 🔊

In this exercise, we're going to give the pick hand a workout. Using the progression from the previous section, A7–D–E7–A7, the arpeggios below feature a four-note pattern that starts on the root of the chord, jumps over a string to play the next note, moves back one (adjacent) string, and then jumps over another string for the final note of the sequence. This pattern is repeated twice per measure while the pick hand alternates downstrokes and upstrokes throughout.

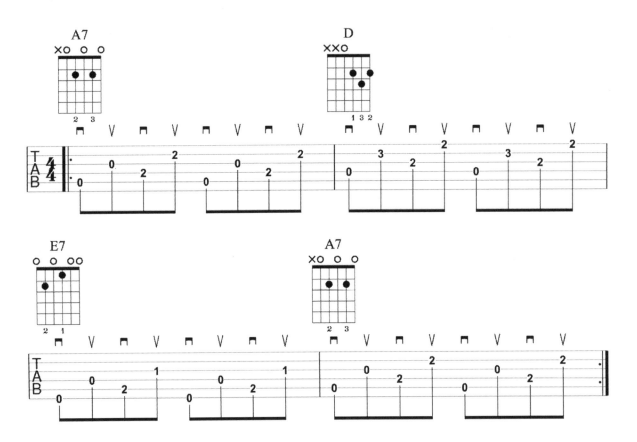

FINGERPICKING (0:45–0:30) 🔊

The fingerpicking pattern in our next exercise is identical to the arpeggio example that we just worked on. However, instead of the pick, we'll be using our pick-hand fingers to execute the arpeggios. The pattern used here, in which the thumb alternates bass-string notes, is referred to as "Travis picking," named after the country picker who made it famous, Merle Travis.

Notice that, as you alternate your thumb on the lowest notes of each chord, the index and middle fingers are each relegated to a single treble string, changing to new strings only when the chords change. Before you attempt the entire exercise, practice the A7 chord in isolation, working to get the pick-hand pattern down cold. Once you achieve that, then you can add in the other chords.

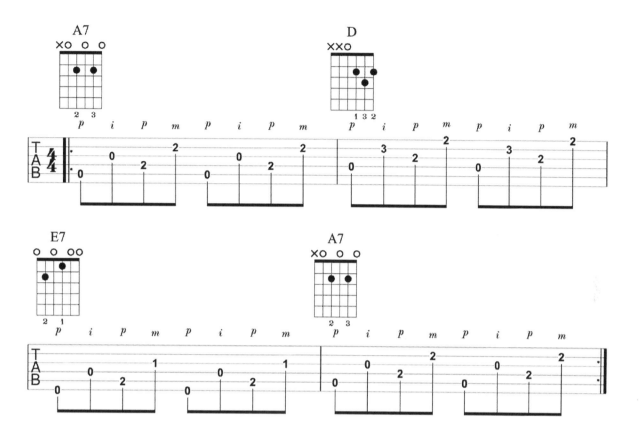

TECHNIQUE: QUARTER-STEP BEND (0:30–0:15) 🔊

Although string bending is considerably more prevalent on electric guitar, it's still an important technique to learn on acoustic. The bends we're going to focus on today are of the quarter-step variety, which sound great when applied to the bass strings in open position, like in our four-bar riff below.

To perform these bends, simply nudge the string downward ever-so-slightly with your fret-hand's middle finger as you pick it. This will cause the string to go slightly out of tune—which is the sound we're going for. But be careful: you don't want to bend the string *too* much. Listen to the audio track to hear how these bends should sound.

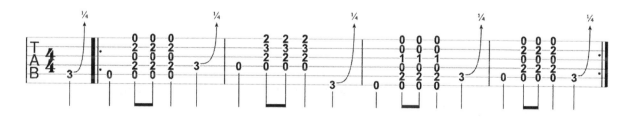

MELODY: WILL THE CIRCLE BE UNBROKEN
(0:15–0:00) 🔊

Today's picking exercise picks up (pardon the pun) where yesterday's left off. Here, string 4 is incorporated once again, but this time, the rhythmic complexity is ratcheted up a notch, incorporating several instances of back-to-back eighth notes. Pluck these eighth-note pairs with downstroke-upstroke combos, as shown in the picking suggestions above the staff.

As for you fret hand, play the notes at fret 2 with your index finger, and the notes at fret 4 with your ring finger. In measures 1–2, when moving from string 3 to string 2, simply roll your index finger downward instead of lifting the finger from the fretboard and reapplying it. In other words, use the index finger as a small, two-string barre.

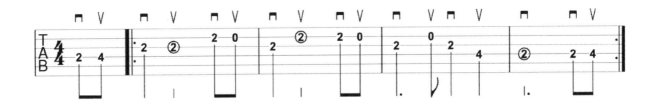

DAY 6

CHORDS: G7, C7 & D7 (1:30–1:15) 🔊

Yesterday, we were introduced to 7th chords—specifically, A7 and E7—and today we're going to learn three more chords of this type: G7, C7, and D7. Let's start with perhaps the easiest of the three, G7. The G7 chord is very similar to the G major chord we've been practicing throughout the week, only the note on string 1 is now played on fret 1 instead of fret 3, which necessitates an adjustment to the fingering. To get the open strings to ring out clearly, you'll need to drop down the wrist of your fretting hand and voice the strings with the very tips of your fingers.

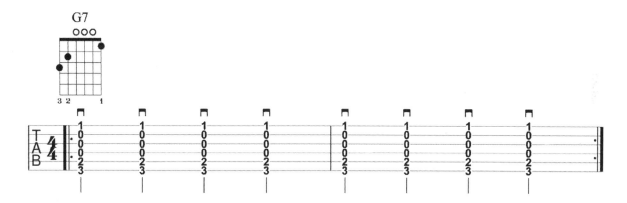

Like G7, the C7 chord below is very similar to its major counterpart, C. The only difference between a standard open C chord and the voicing below is the addition of the pinky to fret 3, string 3. You'll still want to let string 1 ring open, however, so be sure to get those fingers arched!

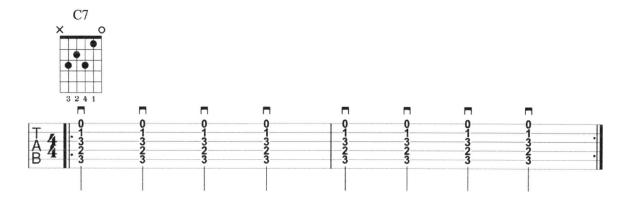

47

The D7 chord below is actually somewhat easier to voice than the standard open D chord. The only difference between the two, note-wise, is the pitch on string 2. Play through this exercise a few times and then move on to the next section, where you'll have an opportunity to test drive all three of these chords some more.

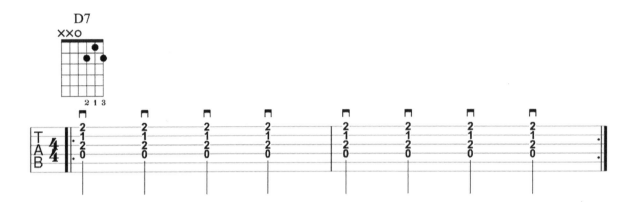

CHORD PROGRESSION: 12-BAR BLUES (1:15–1:00)

One of the most important and most recognizable chord progressions of all time is the 12-bar blues. The *12-bar blues* progression is a 12-measure set of chord changes in which specific chords relative to the song's key occur at specific points in the 12-bar form. Variations of the 12-bar blues exist, but the one on the next page is one of the most common.

Spend the entire 15 minutes of this section playing through the progression several times. A couple of items to keep in mind are the strumming pattern and the rhythm. The strumming pattern features a string of continuous downstrokes, which will give the chord changes a propulsive, or "driving," feel. Also, like much of blues music, this example is played with a *shuffle feel*, which involves making the first eighth note of each eighth-note pair slightly longer than the second. Listen to the audio track to hear how this sounds. You'll likely recognize it right away, because it's a rhythmic feel you've probably heard a thousand times!

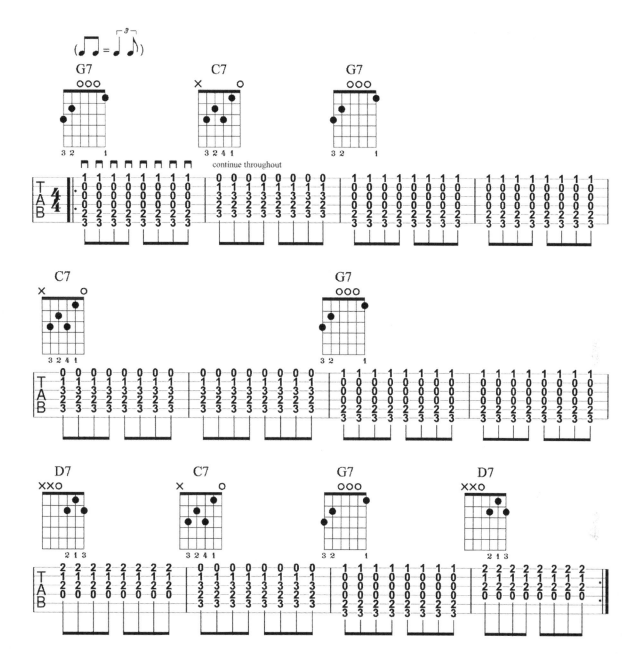

ARPEGGIOS (1:00–0:45) 🔊

This next exercise is written in 12/8 time, meaning each measure contains 12 beats and the eighth note receives each beat. One way to count and feel this time signature is to tap your foot four times per bar—like you would in 4/4 time—and play three notes per beat (these are call *triplets*). Alternatively, you can count and tap your foot on each of the 12 beats, accenting the first eighth note of each three-note (triplet) group: "**1**–2–3–**4**–5–6–**7**–8–9–**10**–11–12," etc. Again, listen to the audio to hear how this sounds.

As for the chords, the voicings used here are the same ones we worked on in the previous two sections. Use three straight downstrokes as the arpeggios ascend, and three straight downstrokes as they descend, paying strict attention to which strings are plucked for each chord.

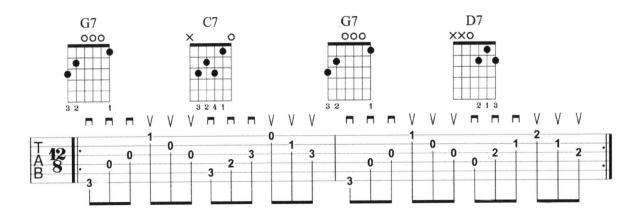

FINGERPICKING (0:45–0:30) 🔊

Now let's fingerpick the arpeggios we just worked on. As you can see, the index, middle, and ring fingers will handle strings 3–1, respectively, while the thumb alternates bass-string notes. The thumb will be a little tricky since it skips a string for the G7 chord but plays adjacent, albeit different, strings for the C7 and D7 chords. Start by playing each chord in isolation a few times, and then try stringing them together. Go slow!

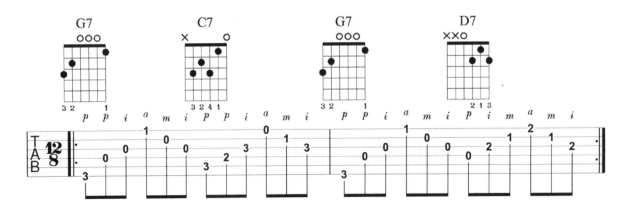

TECHNIQUE: ALTERNATE PICKING (0:30–0:15) 🔊

We've been working on alternate picking since Day 1, but now we're going to practice the technique in a more rigid fashion to build efficiency and speed in your picking hand. In the first exercise below, five notes—E, G, A, B, and D—are looped in an ascending and descending pattern and plucked with strict alternate (down-up, down-up, etc.) picking. Play through this exercise a few times and then try starting with an upstroke: up-down, up-down, etc.

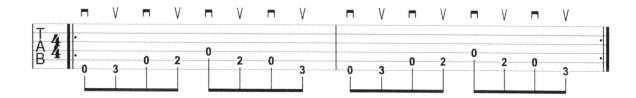

This next exercise is similar to the previous one, only now we're playing on the top strings and *descending* the strings first. Again, use strict alternate picking, starting with a downstroke. Then, once you feel comfortable, try starting with an upstroke.

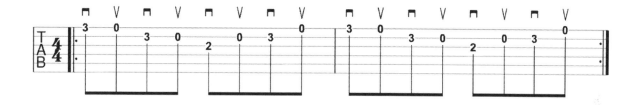

SCALE: E MINOR PENATONIC (0:15–0:00) 🔊

The alternate-picking exercise from the previous section was a preview of what we're going to work on here: the E minor pentatonic scale. Learning this scale will serve two purposes: First, scales are an invaluable resource for composing melodies and playing solos. Second, practicing scales provides an opportunity to further hone your alternate-picking chops.

Notice in the tab below that this scale is simply a combination of the two exercises you practiced in the previous section. However, now we're going to combine them and play through all six strings in ascending and descending order. Remember: use strict alternate picking. As you've probably figured out, the white notes in the scale diagram are the root notes, and the numbers below the tab staff are the fret-hand fingerings: 1 = index, 2 = middle, 3 = ring, and 4 = pinky.

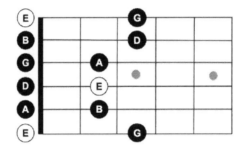

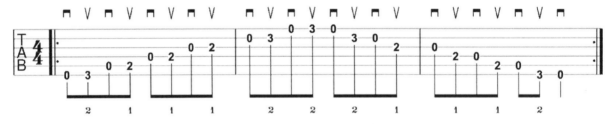

Now that you have the scale at least somewhat under your fingers, let's try the E minor pentatonic guitar lick below. This scale sounds great when soloing over E7 or Em chords, so before you play the lick, which is composed entirely from the E minor pentatonic scale, strum and hold one of those chords, as shown below. This will help your ears identify—and get acclimated to—the sound of the scale relative to the harmony (i.e., chord).

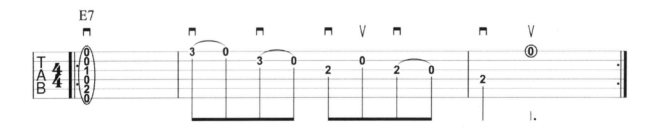

WEEK 1 REVIEW: PUTTING IT ALL TOGETHER (1:30–0:00) 🔊

Congratulations on making through Week 1! To celebrate, we're going to spend today's entire lesson practicing a full song, "When the Saints Go Marching In." Two versions of the song are arranged here. The first arrangement features strummed chords (C, G, and F) throughout, with the strum patterns and chords notated in tab. The second arrangement features the same chords, only the accompaniment is fingerpicked in an eighth-note pattern rather than strummed. The fingerpicked arrangement will probably take more time learn, so divide your practice time accordingly.

The song's melody has also been included in the strummed version so you can practice your alternate-picking chops. You can work on the melody in this session or come back to it later. It's up to you. The squiggly symbol you see in measure 2, 4 and 8 is a *quarter rest*, which indicates one beat of silence, and the small rectangular symbol in measure 12 is a *half rest*, which indicates *two* beats of rest, or silence (these symbols also appear in the three-beat pickup measure).

WHEN THE SAINTS GO MARCHING IN
STRUMMED VERSION

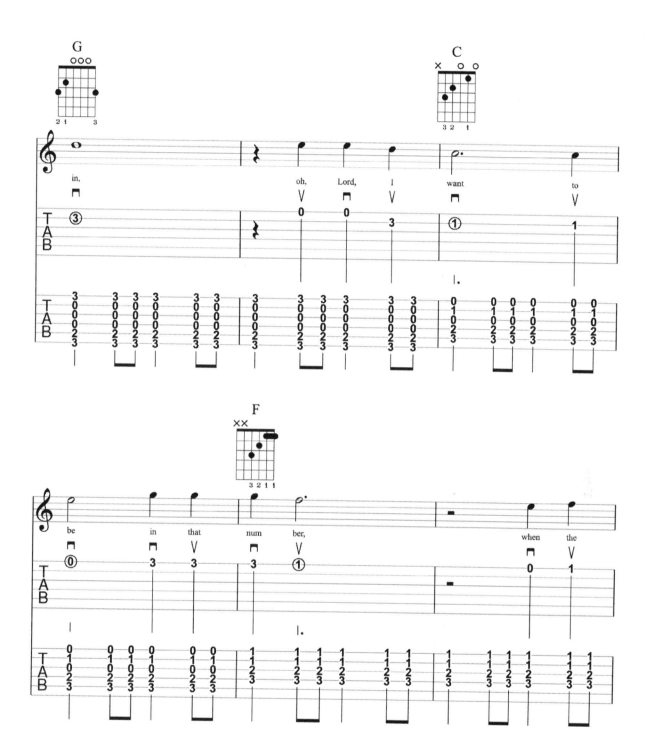

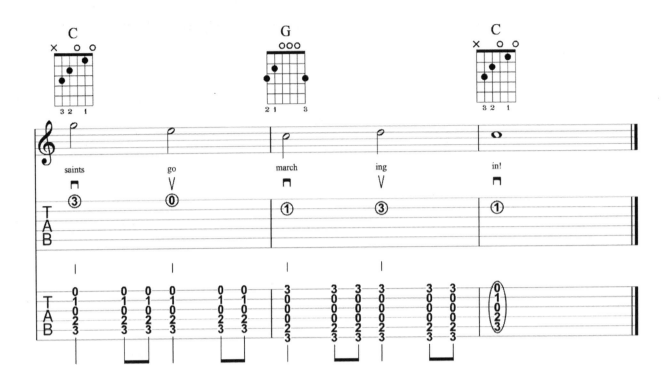

WHEN THE SAINTS GO MARCHING IN
FINGERPICKED VERSION

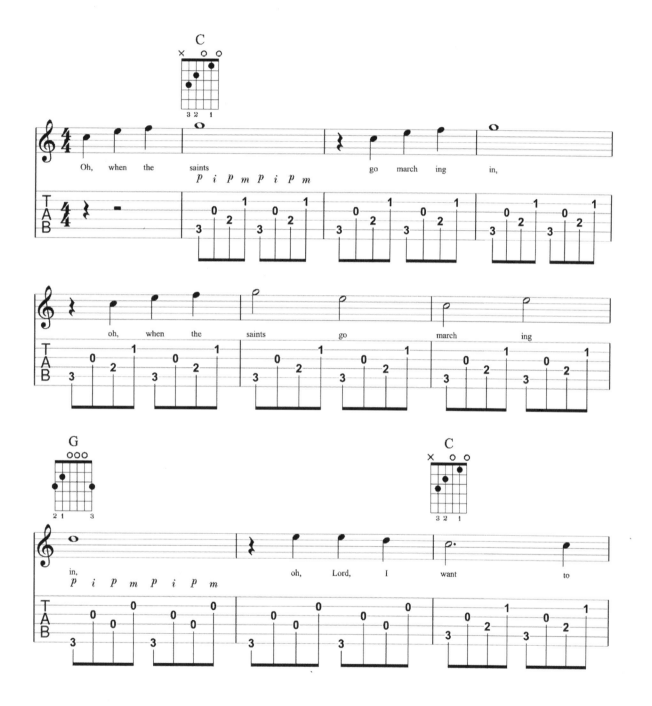

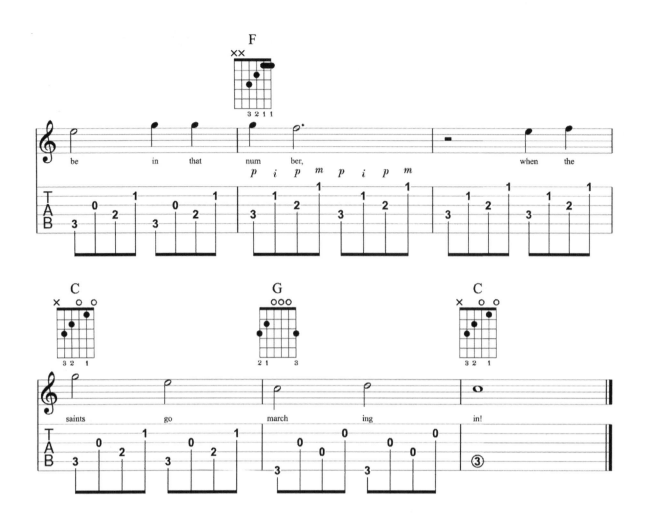

WEEK 2: BARRE CHORDS

The lesson topics we'll be working on this week are holdovers from last week, but most of our focus will now shift from open chords to a more difficult yet important chord type—barre chords. We covered a lot of ground in Week 1, but there's still much more to be covered, so let's get to it.

DAY 8

CHORDS: THREE-STRING BARRE CHORDS (1:30–1:15) ◀))

Over the next four days, we're going to focus intently on common major and minor barre chords, starting with today's three-string shapes and working our way up to full six-string voicings. The plan is to *gradually* increase the number of notes the index finger must barre because, the more robust the barre, the more difficult the chord voicing.

Since open strings are not included in our barre chords, we can move the shapes up and down the fretboard to change keys. Below are three common three-string barre-chord shapes—two major and one minor. The root of the G and Gm voicings is found on string 1, whereas the root of the D chord is found on string 2. Therefore, if you know the names of the notes on those strings, you can move these shapes to play major and minor chords in all 12 keys. Practice the exercise a few times and then see if you can play the same progression in other keys. Use your ears as a guide.

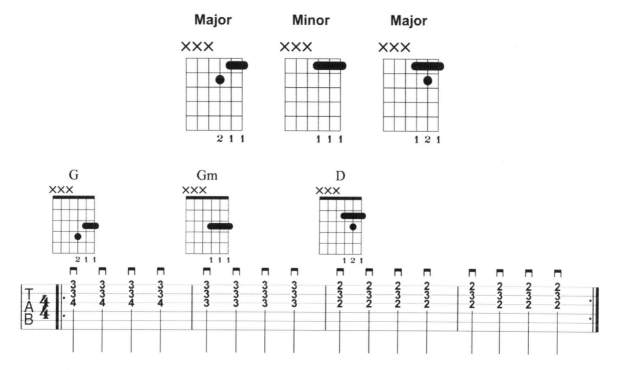

CHORD PROGRESSION: G–Am–D–G (1:15–1:00) 🔊

Now let's take the barre-chord shapes we just learned and apply them to a four-chord progression, G–Am–D–G. This exercise is also our first encounter with 16th notes. A *16th note* has half the rhythmic value of an eighth note; therefore, it takes four 16th notes to equal one beat in 4/4 time, as shown below. Count 16th notes like this: "One-e-&-uh, two-e-&-uh, three-e-&-uh, four-e-&-uh," etc.

Play these 16th notes with a steady stream of alternate (down-up) strumming. As for your fret hand, keep your index finger barred across strings 1–3 throughout the four bars. Even though a three-string barre is note required for the G chord, having it in place will make chord changes more efficient and cleaner (with this approach, the only finger that needs to shift is the middle). Also, depending on which chord you are playing at the moment, use the tip of your fret-hand index or middle finger to mute string 4 while you strum.

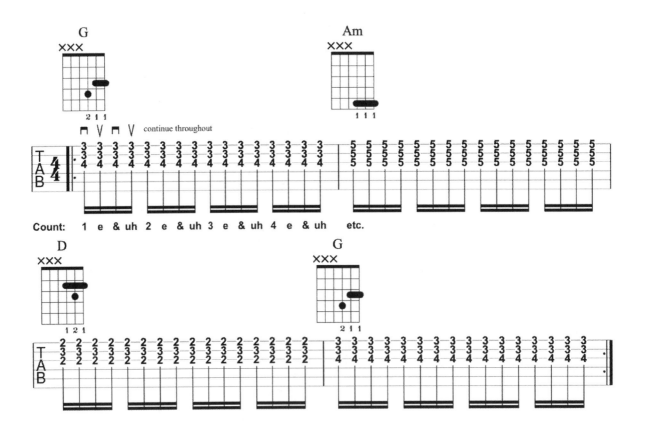

ARPEGGIOS (1:00–0:45) 🔊

Now let's try arpeggiating our three-string barre chords. The exercise below features the G–Am–D–G progression we just learned and is played in a repetitive one-beat arpeggio pattern. Notice the picking sequence: up-up-down-down, up-up-down-down, etc.

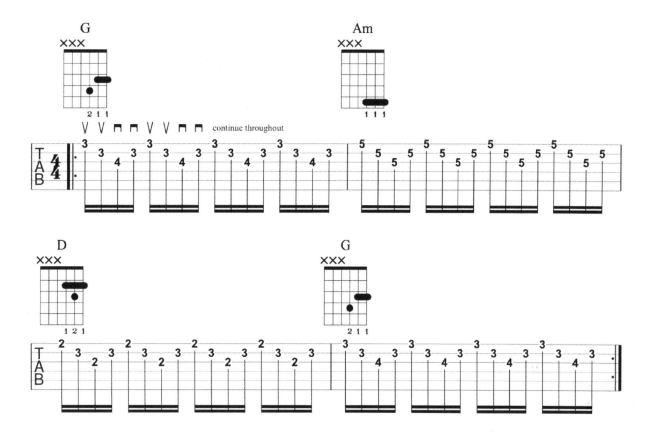

FINGERPICKING (0:45–0:30) 🔊

Now we're going to fingerpick the exercise from the previous section. You can pick this example one of two ways: *m–i–p–i* or *a–m–i–m*. The first pattern, *m–i–p–i*, incorporates the thumb, using it to pluck string 3 while the middle and index handle strings 1 and 2, respectively. Alternatively, the second pattern omits the thumb altogether; instead, using a combination of the ring, middle, and index fingers for strings 1–3, respectively. Try them both, using whichever feels most comfortable to you.

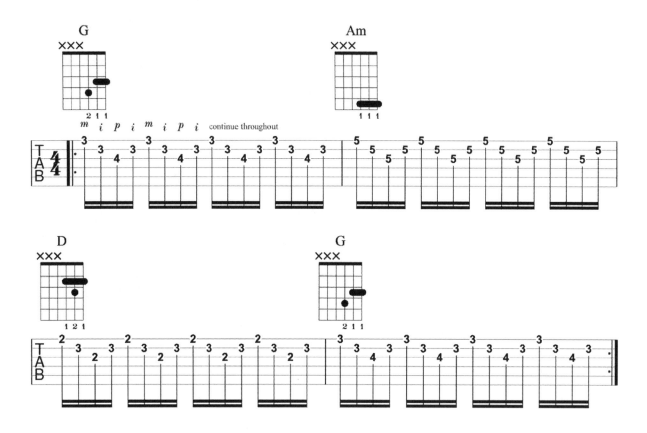

TECHNIQUE: HYBRID PICKING (0:30–0:15) 🔊

In this section, we're going to practice *hybrid picking*, a technique that is equal parts flatpicking and fingerpicking. With this technique, you'll use the pick to pluck strings that, if fingerpicked, would be assigned to the thumb. Meanwhile, the remaining fingers (middle, ring, and pinky) are relegated to picking the higher strings, including plucking multiple strings simultaneously.

The exercise below features the chord progression from the previous three sections but with a new, hybrid-picking pattern. Note that the pick handles the notes on string 3 (much like the thumb in the previous section's exercise), and the middle and ring fingers handle strings 2–1, respectively, including plucking the two strings simultaneously on the "and" of beat 2 in each measure.

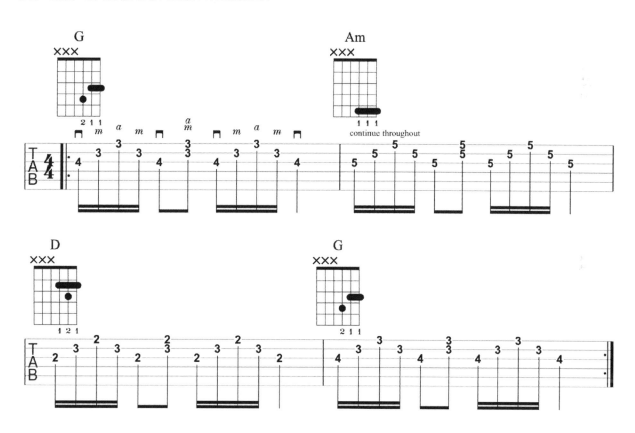

SCALE: E BLUES (0:15–0:00) 🔊

The E blues scale differs from yesterday's E minor pentatonic scale by just one (additional) note, B♭. In our open-position pattern, this note appears in two places: on fret 1, string 5 and on fret 3, string 3. Practice the scale a few times, being sure to follow the fingering suggestions below the tab staff and using strict alternate picking.

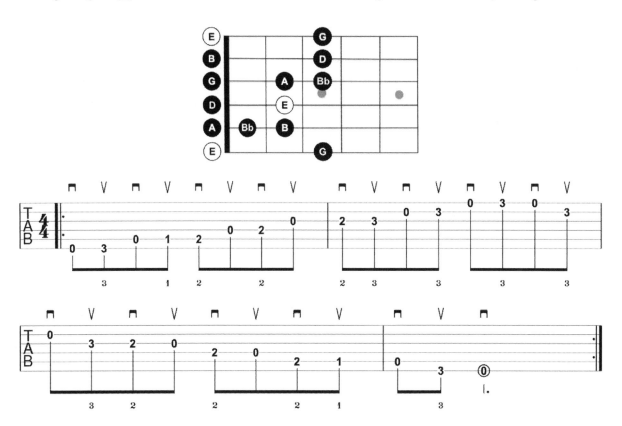

The lick below is derived entirely from the E blue scale pattern that we just practiced. Notice the quarter-step bend on fret 3, string 1 and the inclusion of a hammer-on, two pull-offs, and a legato slide. The slide and pull-off on beat 2 of measure 2 should be performed in one motion; in other words, pick the note at fret 3, string 3, slide down to fret 2, and then pull off to the open string—without repicking the string. Be careful not to rush this three-note sequence—it's very easy to do. Use a metronome and listen to the audio track for guidance.

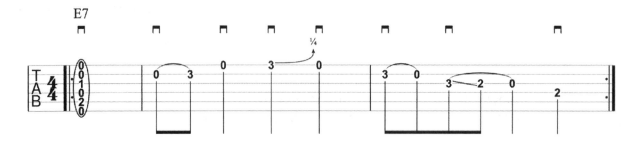

DAY 9

CHORDS: FOUR-STRING BARRE CHORDS (1:30–1:15) 🔊

Today, we're going to add a string to the three-string barre chords that we worked on yesterday. In each of the three voicings below, the ring finger is added to string 4—below the three-string shapes that we already know. The root notes are in the same location, but the addition of string 4 (typically a wound string) gives the chords a little more sonic heft. As you did with the three-string shapes, maintain a three-string index-finger barre as you switch from chord to chord, which will increase fret-hand efficiency and, in turn, reduce unwanted string noise.

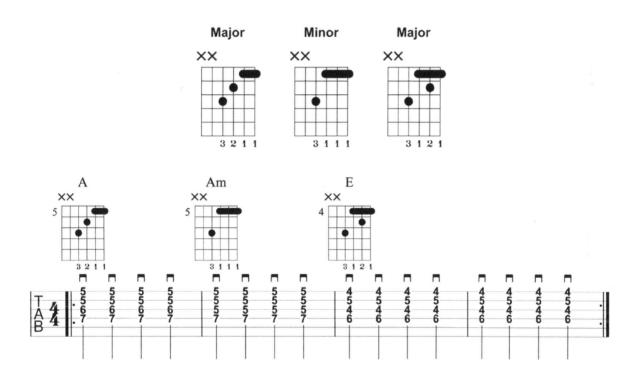

CHORD PROGRESSION: A–E–F♯m–D (1:15–1:00) 🔊

Now let's use our new four-string barre-chord shapes to create a chord progression, A–E–F♯m–D. The rhythm that we're going to use here is a "gallop"—an eighth note followed by two 16ths. This rhythm is counted as follows: "One-&-uh, two-&-uh, three-&-uh, four-&-uh," etc. Also, pay close attention to the strumming pattern, which involves playing back-to-back downstrokes, followed by an upstroke. Essentially, you're going to use alternate (down-up) picking throughout, but on the second 16th note (the "e"), you're going to employ a "ghost" strum; in other words, your strumming arm and wrist will be moving upward but the pick won't make contact with the strings. This will feel awkward at first, but you'll get acclimated to it quickly.

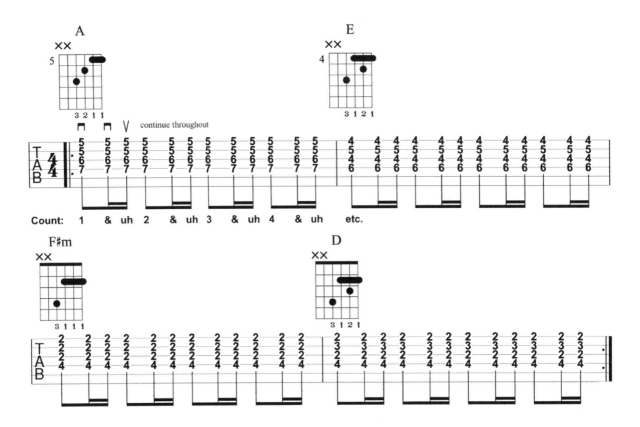

ARPEGGIOS (1:00–0:45) 🔊

In today's arpeggio exercise, we're going to use the chords and rhythm that we just practiced in the previous section. Here, each note of each chord is plucked as you ascend and descend the two-beat pattern (played twice per measure). Use three consecutive downstrokes on the way up, and three consecutive upstrokes on the way down.

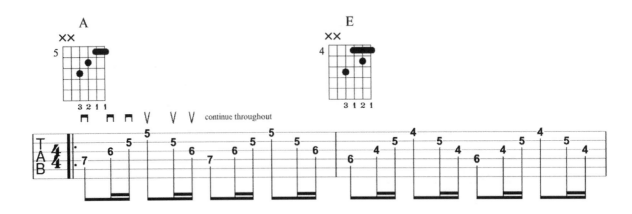

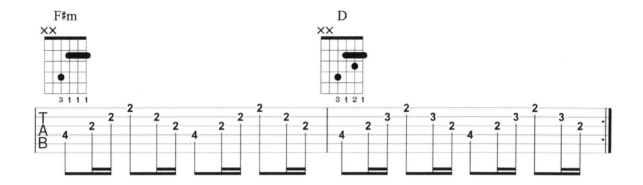

FINGERPICKING (0:45–0:30) 🔊

Now let's fingerpick the arpeggios that we just learned in the previous section. The pick-hand pattern we're going to use throughout is *p–i–m–a–m–i.* The thumb will handle all the notes on string 4 while the index, middle, and ring fingers cover the notes on string 3–1, respectively.

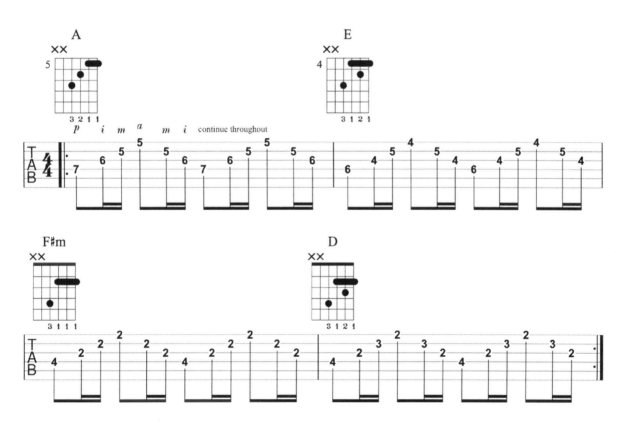

TECHNIQUE: NATURAL HARMONICS (0:30–0:15)

Natural harmonics are a great technique to get familiar with because they can add a nice texture to chord fills or perfectly punctuate a lead line in your solos. Playing harmonics requires a technique that differs from regularly fretted notes. Instead of placing the fingertip directly onto the string and pressing it to fretboard, make gentle contact with the string—without applying pressure—directly over the metal fret *wire* and then pluck it. The result should be a high-pitched bell-like tone (listen to the audio track).

In the example below, gently lay your index finger across the wire at fret 12, making contact with the string without pressing it to the fretboard. Pluck each string with a downstroke and allow the harmonics to ring out. In measures 2 and 3, shift your fret hand to fret 7 and fret 5, respectively, and do the same.

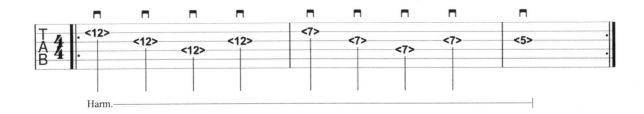

This next example is similar to the first but now we'll be plucking two harmonics simultaneously at frets 12, 7, and 5. Again, be sure to place your finger directly over the fret *wire* to produce the harmonics.

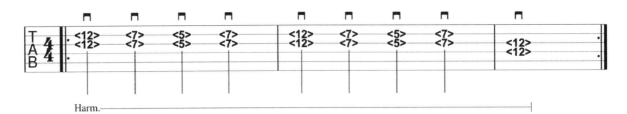

SCALE: G MAJOR PENTATONIC (0:15–0:00) 🔊

The great thing about learning a new scale is that, instead of learning one scale, you're actually learning two! That's because every minor scale has a relative major, and vice versa. In music theory, the term "relative" means scales that share the same notes, only starting on different pitches, or roots. For example, our E minor pentatonic scale (E–G–A–B–D) from Day 6 also has a relative major, G *major* pentatonic (G–A–B–D–E). Both scales share the same notes; they just start on different pitches (roots).

Since you're already familiar with the pattern, getting comfortable with G major pentatonic shouldn't take long. Just remember to use strict alternate picking throughout.

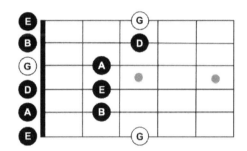

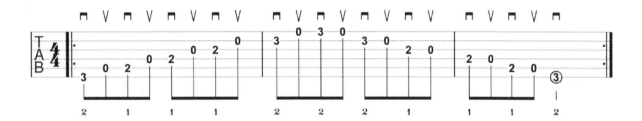

Now let's apply our new scale to a lick. Start by strumming the G chord and then play through the two-bar phrase. Again, by playing the chord first, your ears will learn to hear how the scale sounds relative to the harmony (chord).

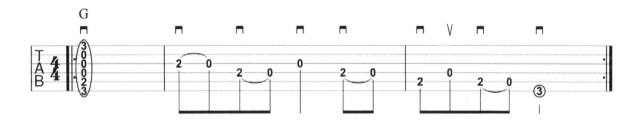

CHORDS: FIVE-STRING BARRE CHORDS (1:30–1:15)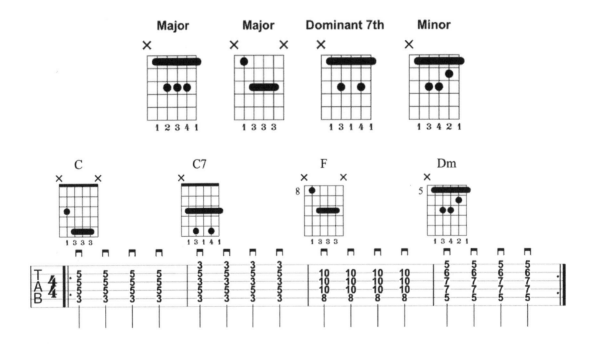

This is the point where our barre-chord studies get considerably more challenging. So, if you find yourself struggling with these shapes, don't get discouraged—they're not easy! Just try to do your best with each exercise and move on to the next section when the time is up. This is a better strategy than trying to perfect each exercise before moving on, as it'll limit frustration and keep you motivated. You can always come back to these exercise on another day.

The five-string barre-chord shapes we'll be working on today are illustrated in the chord frames below. I've included two version of the major chord because the first (five-string) version is impractical, so guitarists tend to favor the easier four-string version, although the ring-finger barre presents its own challenges. The root notes for these chords are located on string 5; therefore, if you memorize the notes on that string, you'll be able to play these chords in all 12 keys. Spend 15 minutes playing through the exercise and getting acclimated to these shapes and then move on to the Chord Progression section.

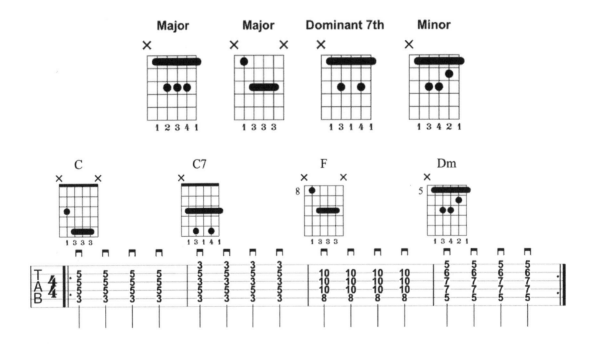

CHORD PROGRESSION: Em–D–C–B7 (1:15–1:00)

Now we're going use our new five-string barre-chord shapes to create a new chord progression, Em–D–C–B7. The rhythm that we're going to use here is a "reverse gallop"—two 16th notes followed by a single eighth note. This rhythm is counted as follows: "One-e-&, two-e-&, three-e-&, four-e-&," etc. The strumming pattern used here is somewhat similar to the one we used yesterday, only now the back-to-back downstrokes occur when moving from one beat to the next, rather than on the middle of the beat. So, you'll still be alternate (down-up) strumming throughout, but on the last 16th note of each beat (the "uh"), you're going to use a ghost strum.

Take this one very slow at first and be sure to count as you strum. If the chords give you trouble, practice each one in isolation before stringing them together.

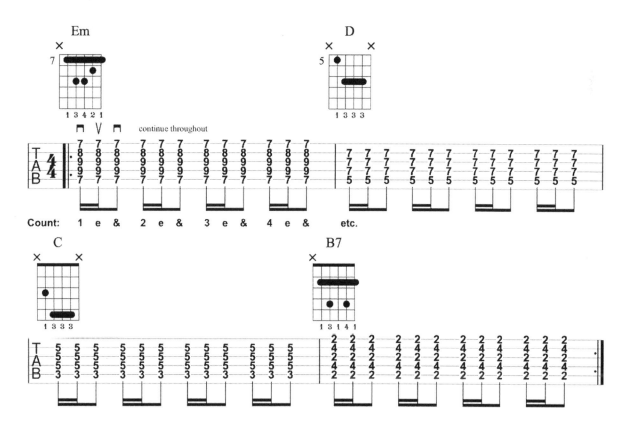

ARPEGGIOS (1:00–0:45) 🔊

Now let's arpeggiate the chord progression that we just learned in the previous section, using the same rhythm. Like yesterday's arpeggio exercise, this one utilizes continuous downstrokes as we ascend the arpeggio, and continuous upstrokes as we descend. Practice each chord in isolation before attempting to play the entire progression.

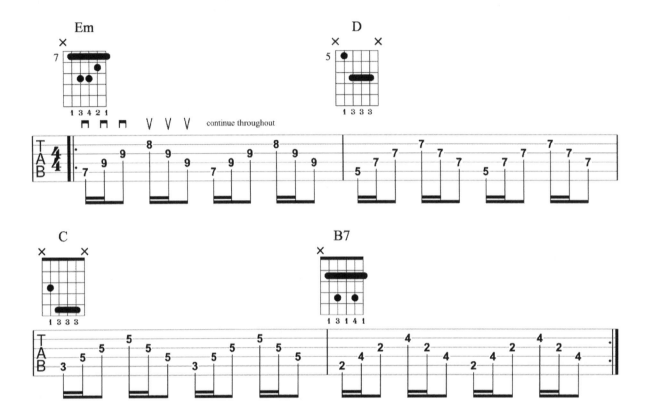

FINGERPICKING (0:45–0:30) 🔊

As we've done throughout the book, now we're going to fingerpick the arpeggio exercise that we just practiced. The fingerpicking pattern used here, *p–i–m–a–m–i,* is identical to the one used yesterday, only the rhythm and strings are different. Here, we'll use the thumb to pluck all the notes on string 5, and the index, middle, and ring fingers to pluck the notes on string 4–2, respectively. Again, don't hesitate to practice each chord separately before attempting to play the entire progression—in fact, I encourage it.

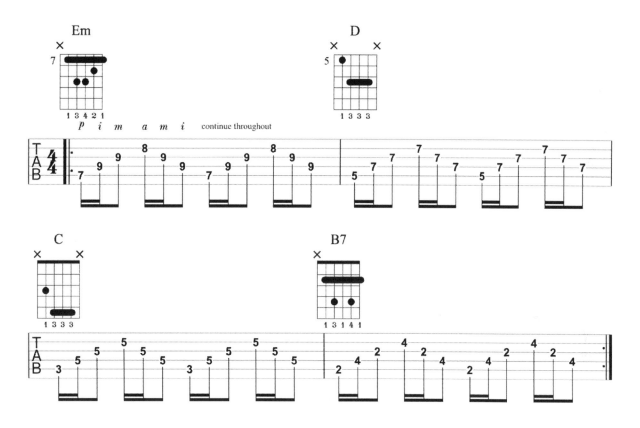

TECHNIQUE: DOUBLE STOPS (0:30–0:15)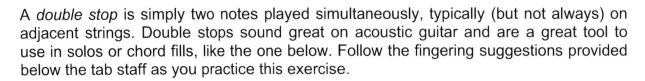

A *double stop* is simply two notes played simultaneously, typically (but not always) on adjacent strings. Double stops sound great on acoustic guitar and are a great tool to use in solos or chord fills, like the one below. Follow the fingering suggestions provided below the tab staff as you practice this exercise.

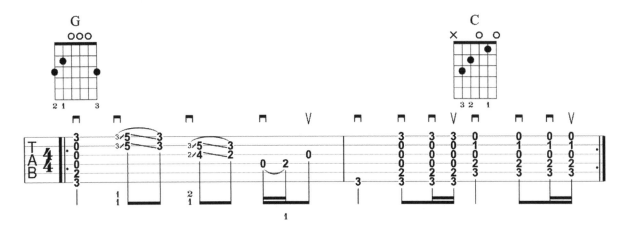

For this next example, use your fret-hand's pinky to perform the first hammer-on in measure 1, and your middle finger for the other two. Let the notes ring out as you move through the double stops.

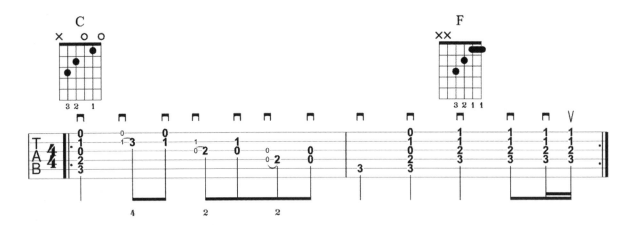

SCALE: G MAJOR (0:15–0:00)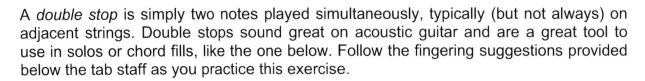

So far, we've spent our time working on five-note pentatonic scales (as well as the six-note E blues scale). Today, we're going to learn our first *seven*-note scale, G major. The major scale is the cornerstone of Western music (the music we listen to and play).

The G major scale differs from the G major *pentatonic* scale by just two (additional) notes: C and F♯. If you look closely at the diagram below, you'll notice that all the notes

74

of G major pentatonic are present, but now the two extra notes (C and F♯) are included. Because of the similarities, getting acclimated to this new scale should be relatively easy. As with all our scales, use strict alternate strumming throughout. After 7–8 minutes, move onto the guitar lick.

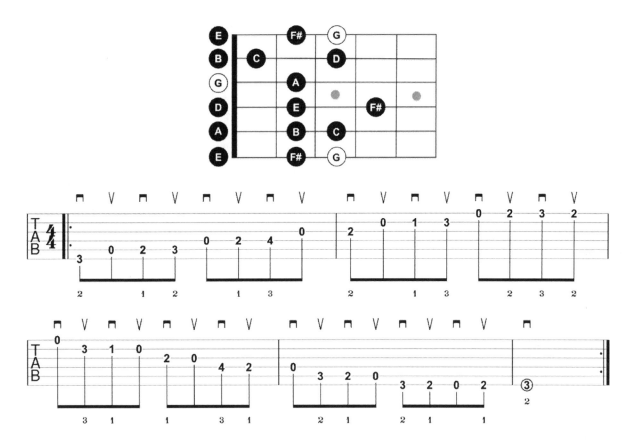

This guitar lick is derived entirely from the G major scale that we just learned. It's played in a bluegrass style and requires strict alternating picking. Be sure to use your metronome for this one!

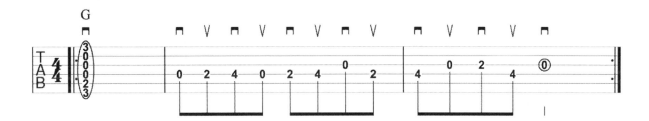

CHORDS: SIX-STRING BARRE CHORDS (1:30–1:15) 🔊

After three days of pretty intense barre-chord work, we've arrived at our toughest challenge yet: six-string shapes. Barring across all six strings of the guitar takes strength and stamina in the fretting hand, which is why we've been working up to these shapes, one string at a time. Hopefully, the work you've put in will make learning these new chords considerably easier than if we hand just started with them.

The six-string barre-chord shapes we'll be working on today are illustrated in the chord frames below. The root notes for these chords are located on string 6; therefore, if you memorize the notes on that string, you'll be able to play these chords in all 12 keys. The voicings for each of the three chord types—major, minor, and dominant 7th—are similar, so once you're able to get the major shape under your fingers, the other two shouldn't give you too much trouble. For example, to change the major shape to minor, simply lift your middle finger from the fretboard. Similarly, to change from major to dominant, simply remove your pinky from string 4.

Practice the F–Gm–B♭–C7 progression below several times. Notice that, unlike open-position chord progressions, using these shapes exclusively requires you to cover a lot of fretboard territory.

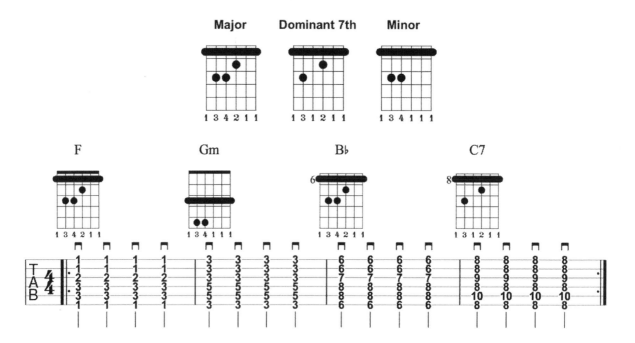

CHORD PROGRESSION: Gm–F–B♭–C7 (1:15–1:00) 🔊

Now let's take the four chords from our previous progression—F, Gm, B♭, and C7—and create a new progression: Gm–F–B♭–C7. The rhythm we'll be using is a combination of quarter notes, the gallop, the reverse gallop, and a new one—a dotted eighth note followed by a 16th. If you remember, a dot increases a note's duration by one half of its original value; therefore, a dotted eighth note has a rhythmic value of 3/4 of a beat (1/2 + 1/4 = 3/4). When you add the 16th note (on the "uh"), you get a full beat (3/4 + 1/4 = 1). Due to the disparity in rhythms, you'll want to closely follow the picking directions notated above the staff.

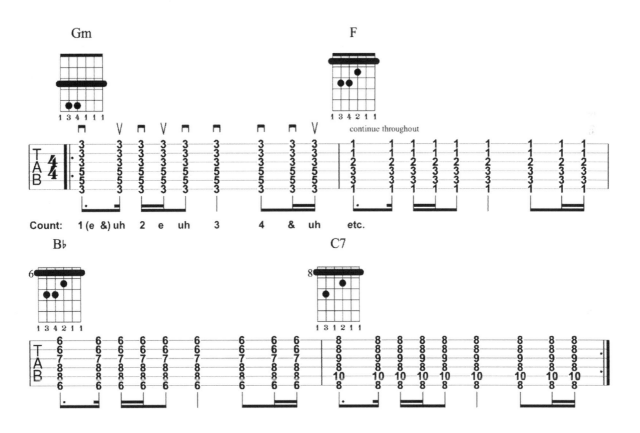

ARPEGGIOS (1:00–0:45) 🔊

The biggest challenges when performing this arpeggio pattern is making the chord changes (naturally) and plucking the right strings. As you can see, the four-beat pattern goes from plucking five adjacent strings on beats 1–2 to plucking non-adjacent strings on beats 3–4. Fortunately, the picking pattern is pretty straightforward: use downstrokes exclusively, except for the notes on string 2. Be sure to listen to the audio to hear how this one sounds.

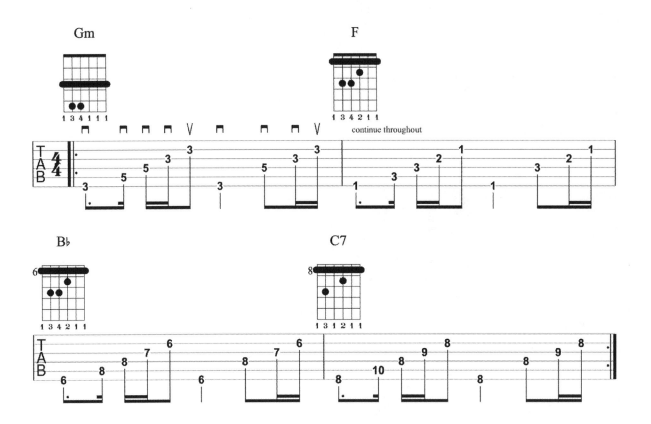

FINGERPICKING (0:45–0:30) 🔊

Fingerpicking this exercise might actually be easier than picking it because your thumb won't have to skip a string on beats 3–4 of each measure; instead, the index, middle, and ring fingers remain on strings 4–2 throughout, with the thumb covering the notes on strings 5 and 6. (These chord shapes can cause a lot of soreness and fatigue in the fretting hand, especially for beginner guitarists, so feel free to take a break, whether it's for 10 minutes or the rest of the day.)

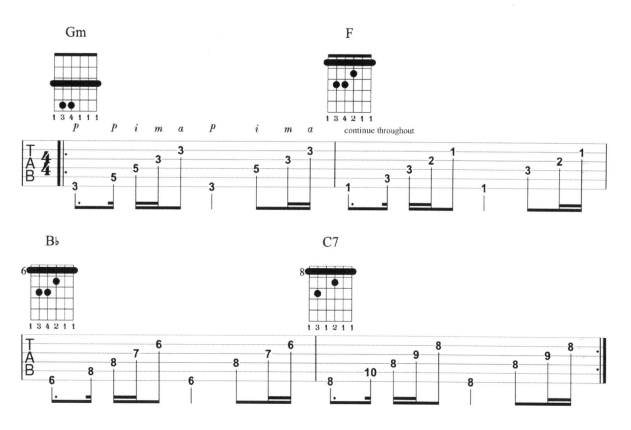

TECHNIQUE: PALM MUTING (0:30–0:15) 🔊

Sometimes we don't want certain notes to ring out when we pluck them; we want to produce a percussive thud. One way to achieve this to use palm muting. As the term suggests, *palm muting* involves using the palm of our picking hand to mute the string at the same time it's being plucked, resulting in a deadened string attack.

On guitar, the most popular application of palm muting occurs on the bass strings, particularly string 6. To hear this in technique in action, play through the exercise below, which incorporates sixth-string palm muting into the Gm–F–Bb–C7 progression we've been working on today. To execute the palm mutes, simply rest the fleshy "blade" of your pick hand on the string as you pluck it. Then, when it's time to strum the chords, lift your hand from the string, strum the chord, then reapply the hand for the subsequent palm mutes. Use downstrokes throughout the exercise.

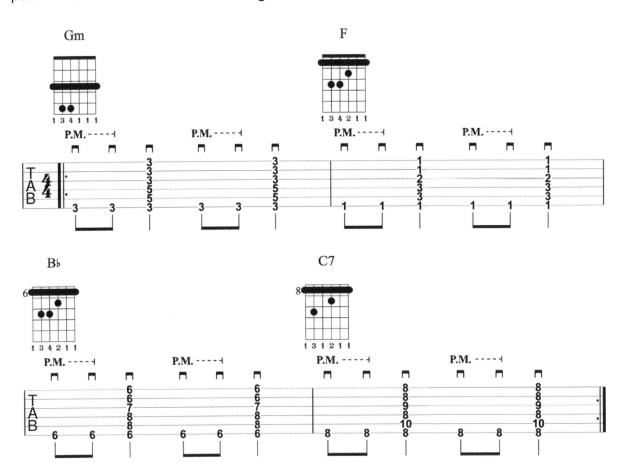

Once you get a handle on the first exercise, you can try your hand—literally—on this next palm-muting exercise. This one is a little more complex, as it requires you to pluck a gallop rhythm while the hand mutes the string. Use a down-down-up picking combo for the palm-muted beats.

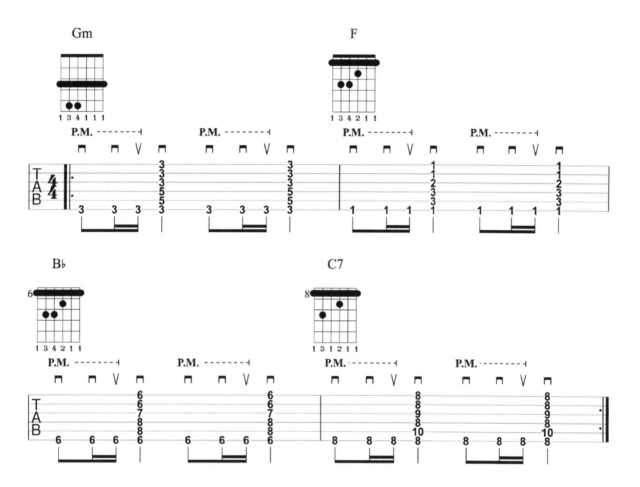

SCALE: A MINOR PENTATONIC (0:15–0:00) 🔊

We've spent the past several days learning various scales in open position—E minor pentatonic, G major pentatonic, E blues, etc.—and now we're going to learn one more, A minor pentatonic. This time, however, we're going to be playing a scale that starts on a string other than string 6.

The scale pattern below starts on A, the root of the A minor pentatonic scale, which also happens to be the open fifth string. This pattern is a little more awkward to finger in the fretting hand, so be sure to follow the fingering suggestions below the staff. Practice the scale several times and then put it into action by playing the accompanying guitar lick.

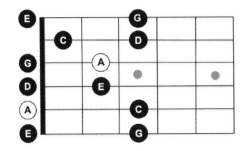

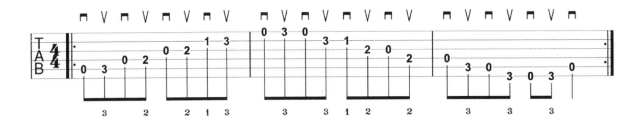

This lick is pretty straightforward in that it moves straight up and down the lower portion of the scale (strings 5–3). To give the phrase its proper feel, be sure to incorporate all of the notated techniques: hammer-ons, pull-offs, and quarter-step bend.

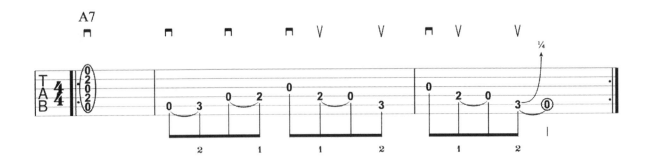

CHORDS: MAJOR 7TH & MINOR 7TH
(1:30–1:15) 🔊

Over the past week and a half, we've devoted a fair bit of time to learning dominant 7th chords in open position and as barre chords. Today, we're going to learn the other two common 7th-chord types: major 7th and minor 7th.

Major 7th and minor 7th chords can be voiced a number of different ways, but we're going to focus on some of the most common, which are illustrated in the chord frames below. As you can see, some of these chords are similar to the barre-chord shapes that we've already learned, and some are voiced on non-adjacent strings. Spend a few minutes familiarizing yourself with these new voicings before moving on to the exercise—a Cmaj7–Am7–Dm7–G7 progression featuring three of these new shapes, plus a dominant 7th voicing you already know.

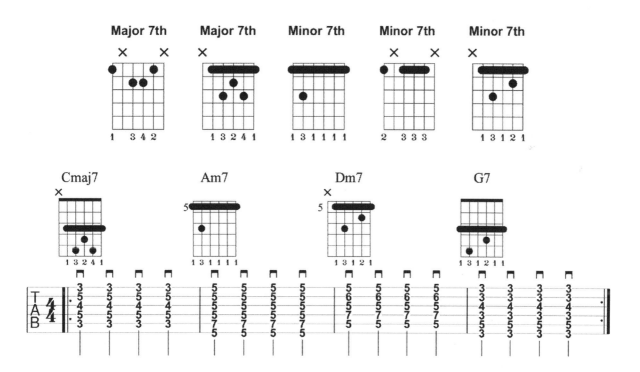

CHORD PROGRESSION: Gmaj7–Am7–Bm7–Am7 (1:15–1:00) 🔊

This next exercise is written in 6/8 time, meaning each measure contains *six* beats and the eighth note receives each beat. This is similar to the 12/8 time signature that we learned back on Day 6, only now each measure contains half as many beats. To feel this time signature, tap your foot twice per bar, counting "**1**–2–3–**4**–5–6," etc.

As for the chords, the voicings used here are the two unused voicings from the previous section. These voicings will take some time to get used to, particularly learning how to properly mute strings 5 and 1—the strings not incorporated into the chord—with the fret hand while simultaneously voicing the chord. To give this exercise its proper feel, strum all of the eighth notes with a downstroke (no upstrokes here!).

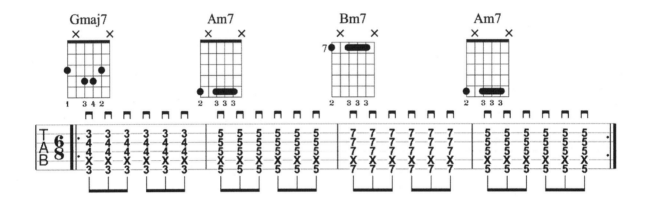

ARPEGGIOS (1:00–0:45) 🔊

Now let's try arpeggiating the major 7th and minor 7th chords from the previous section. In the exercise below, the arpeggio pattern is pretty straightforward: use downstrokes as you ascend the chord, and upstrokes as you descend. The trickiest part of this pattern is the string skip that occurs at the beginning of each measure—skipping from string 6 to string 4—but we've encountered this type of maneuver several times in the past, so it shouldn't give you too much trouble.

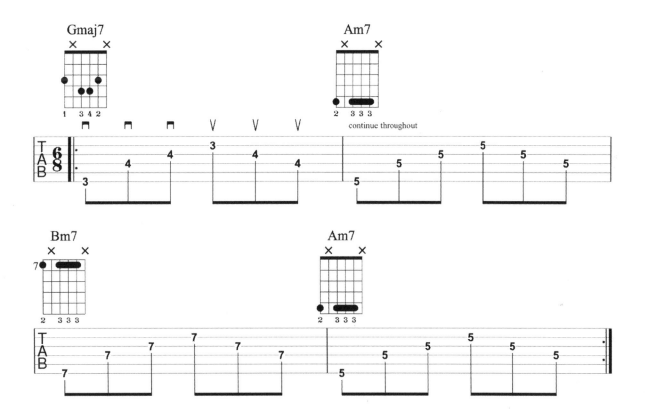

FINGERPICKING (0:45–0:30) 🔊

The fingerpicking pattern used in this exercise, *p–i–m–a–m–i*, is one we've used previously, so you shouldn't have too much trouble getting acclimated to it. As you can see, the thumb is in change of the notes on string 6, while the index, middle, and ring fingers pluck strings 4–2, respectively, all the way through the exercise. The straightforward nature of the picking will allow you to focus much of your attention on the real challenge: voicing and changing chords.

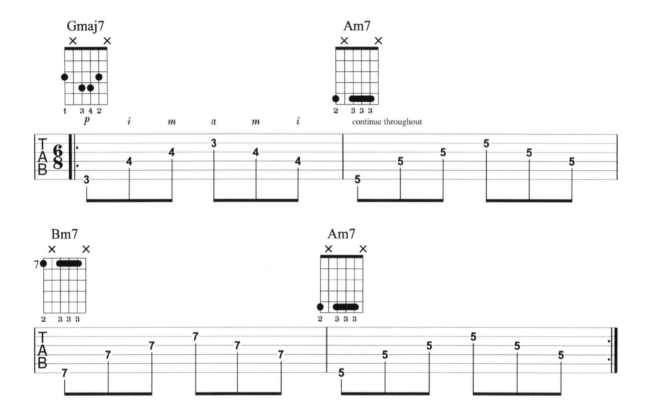

TECHNIQUE: PERCUSSIVE THUMB SLAPS (0:30–0:15) 🔊

One style of acoustic guitar that has seen a lot of growth in popularity the past two decades is percussive playing, particularly thumb slaps in the style of John Mayer. *Percussive thumb slaps* involve striking a bass string (usually string 6) with the pick-hand thumb on beats 2 and 4 of each measure to mimic a snare drum. This enables the guitarists to add a percussive element to their chord playing, which is particularly useful and desirable in a solo setting.

The example below is played entirely fingerstyle, using the chords from our previous exercises. In each measure, the full chord is plucked on beat 1, the pick-hand thumb slaps string 6 on beat 2, and then the chord is re-plucked on the "and" of beat 2 and held though beat 3. (Those slurs are called *ties*, which connect two or more notes of the same pitch and indicate that they are to be played as a single note; in other words, their rhythmic values are combined.) Then, on beat 4, the thumb slaps string 6 once more to complete the snare-drum backbeat. This pattern is repeated for the remaining two chords, Am7 and Bm7.

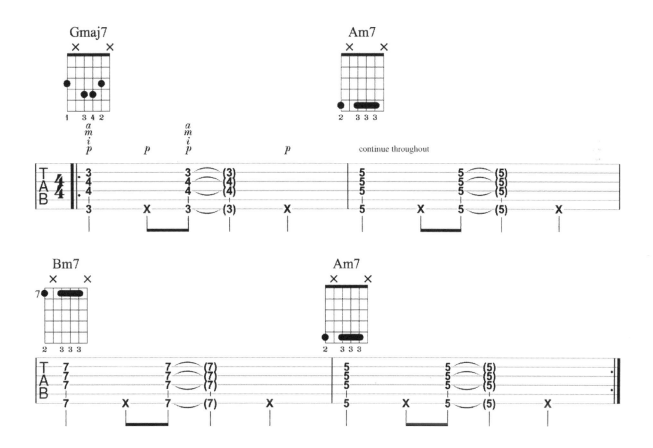

If the previous exercise didn't give you too much trouble, try your hand at the one below, which features a bit more *syncopation*, or accents on weak beats. For example, after plucking the chord on beat 1, the upper portion of the voicing is re-plucked on the last 16th note of the beat (the "uh"). Additionally, string 6 (the root) is plucked on the "and" of beat 2 and the upper portion of the voicing is plucked directly on beat 3. Notice how these slight changes in articulation make a significant difference with respect to the groove and vibe of this example.

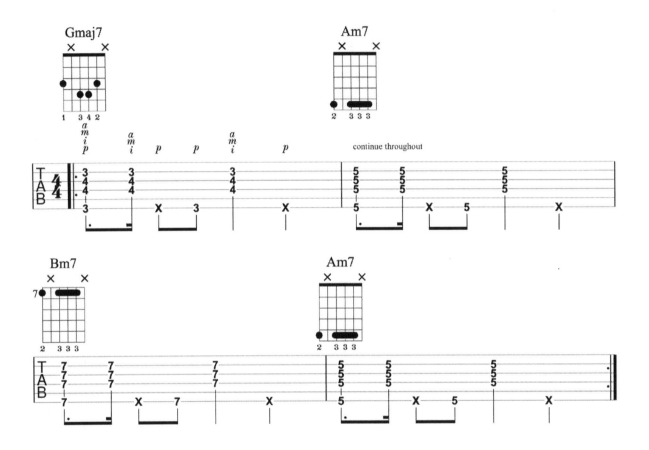

SCALE: A BLUES (0:15–0:00) 🔊

Yesterday, we learned the A minor pentatonic scale, and today we're going to learn its six-note counterpart, the A blues scale. The A blues scale differs from the A minor pentatonic scale by just one (additional) note, E♭. In our open-position pattern below, this note appears in two places: on fret 1, string 4 and on fret 4, string 2. Practice the scale a few times, following the fingering suggestions below the tab staff and using strict alternate picking.

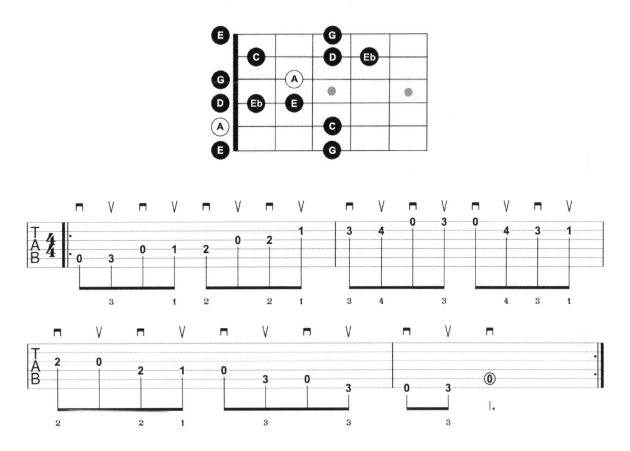

This country-style A blues scale lick sounds great over A7 or Am chords. Use the fingering suggestions below the staff to help with your performance—and don't overlook the pull-offs, slide, and quarter-step bend. If you have trouble, listen to the audio to hear how this lick should sound.

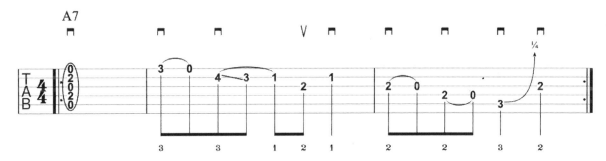

CHORDS: SUSPENDED (1:30–1:15) 🔊

Suspended, or "sus," chords are a popular alternative to regular major or minor chords—and are often played in concert with one another. The example below illustrates how suspended chords are commonly used in conjunction with their major counterparts. Spend a few minutes playing through each of the two-bar phrases below. What you'll notice is that moving from major to sus2 (suspended 2nd) or sus4 (suspended 4th) simply requires adding or removing a finger to the original (major) chord.

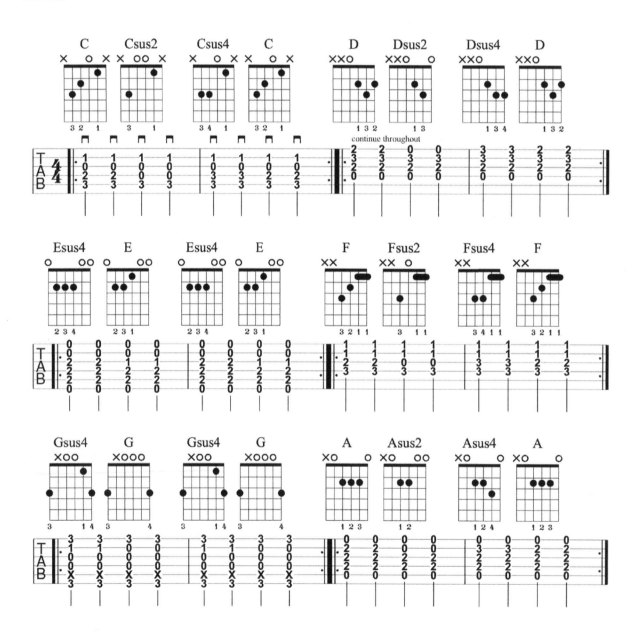

CHORD PROGRESSION: A–D–E–A (1:15–1:00) 🔊

In the exercise below, we're going to use sus2 and sus4 chords to add melodic interest to an otherwise mundane A–D–E–A progression. Notice how much more sophisticated and interesting the progression sounds by adding a sus chord here and there. Although it sounds like a progression composed of more than four chords, the harmony never deviates from the fundamental A–D–E–A changes.

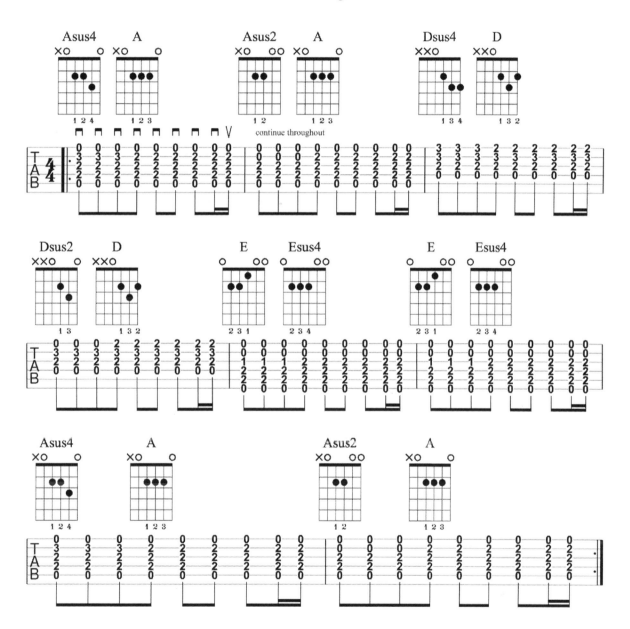

91

ARPEGGIOS (1:00–0:45)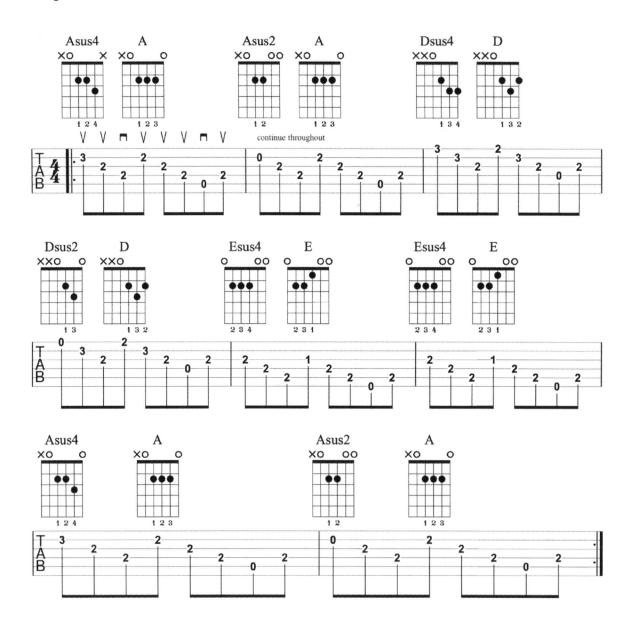

Now let's hear how these sus chords sound when they're arpeggiated along with their major counterparts. The exercise below follows the same changes as the previous example, but now the chords are plucked in a series of (mostly) descending arpeggios. These arpeggios can be a little tricky, so be sure to use the suggested picking pattern as a guide. And take it slow!

FINGERPICKING (0:45–0:30) 🔊

Now let's try fingerpicking our sus chord exercise. The main takeaway from this exercise is the "pinch" technique, which is utilized on beat 1 and the "and" of beat 2 of each measure. A *pinch* involves plucking two notes simultaneously, typically with the thumb and either the index, middle, or ring finger. Notice that, when the chords change, a pinch is used to accent the change and drive home the sound of the new harmony (chord). The same fingerpicking pattern is used throughout, but you'll need to shift it two a new set of strings for each chord change.

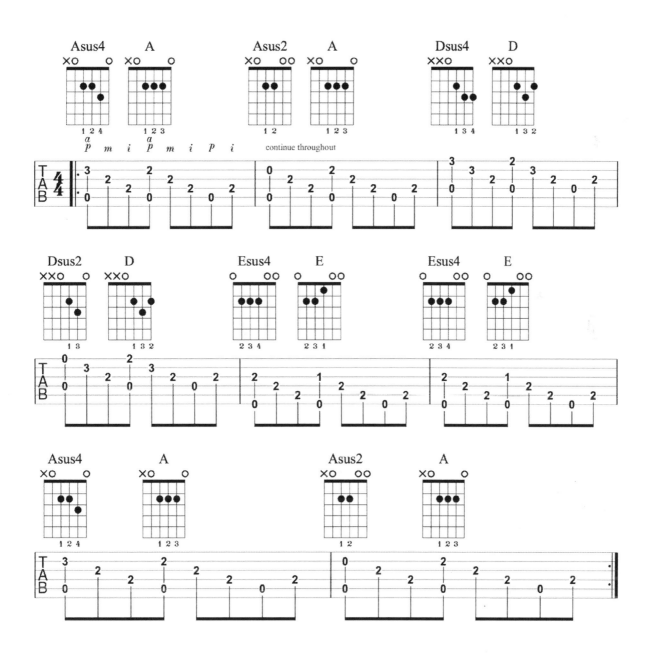

TECHNIQUE: CHORD EMBELLISHMENT (0:30–0:15)

Since were on the topic of sus chords, it's a good time to bring up chord embellishment (sus chords are frequently used to "embellish" chords). Like the sus chord exercises we've been playing, *chord embellishment* is a way to add more color and interest to a progression—without changing the fundamental chord changes.

In the exercise below, "color" chords (sus and add9), hammer-ons, and pull-offs are used to embellish the chords of a D–C–G–D progression. Hammer-ons and pull-offs are a great way to introduce movement to an otherwise static chord, as well as to quickly move between major and sus chords. The ties in this example create a lot of syncopation (accents on weak beats), so be sure to listen to the audio track for help with performing this exercise.

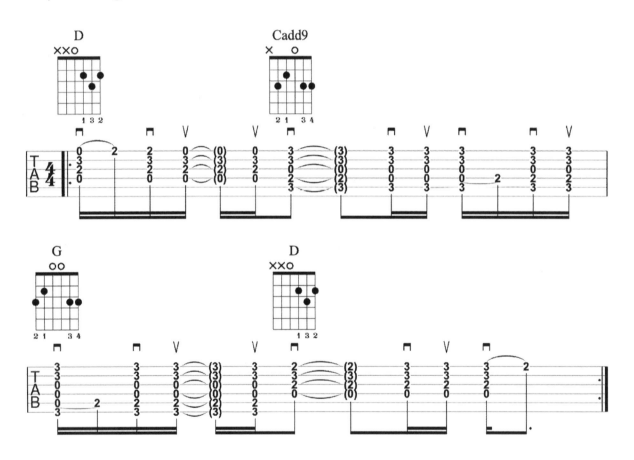

SCALE: C MAJOR PENTATONIC (0:15–0:00)

Just as G major pentatonic is the relative major of E minor pentatonic, C major pentatonic (C–D–E–G–A) is the relative major of A minor pentatonic (A–C–D–E–G), the scale we learned on Day 11. As such, the fingering below is identical to A minor pentatonic, only now we're starting on C, the root of our new scale. As always, follow the fingering suggestions below the tab staff and use strict alternate picking throughout.

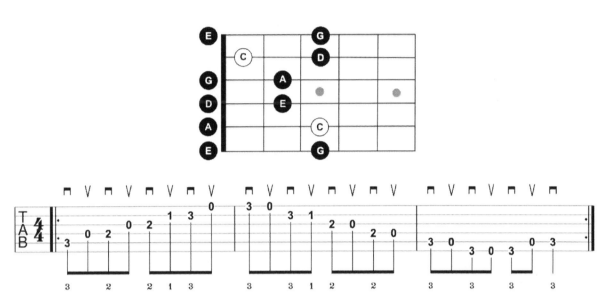

The C major pentatonic lick below has a strong country and bluegrass vibe. Take it slow at first and be sure to incorporate the hammer-ons and pull-offs, which will help tremendously in performing the lick.

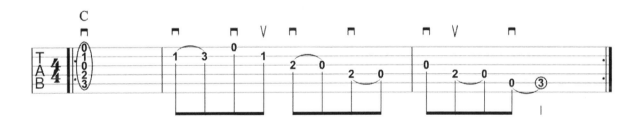

DAY 14

WEEK 2 REVIEW: PUTTING IT ALL TOGETHER (1:30–0:00) 🔊

You did it! You made it to Day 14, the final day of our two-week acoustic guitar journey! We've covered a lot of ground over the course of these 14 days, so we're going to use our final 90 minutes to review some of the material we've learned.

Like Day 7, we're going to eschew short, four-bar exercises in favor of a full song, "Battle Hymn of the Republic," for our weekly review. Once again, two versions of the song are presented here, one a strummed barre-chord arrangement, and the other a fingerpicked arrangement. Both versions featuring the same four chords (C, F, Am, and G) and both are played in 6/8 time, which we covered on Day 12.

The song's melody has also been proved in the strumming arrangement so you can practice your alternate picking. Granted, 90 minutes will probably be inefficient time to practice all three techniques—flatpicking, strumming, and fingerpicking—but choose which one you prefer to practice first, then come back and tackle the others later. As you know by now, barre chords are not easy, so don't get discouraged if this song takes you longer to learn than "When the Saints Go Marching In" did. It's to be expected. Just do your best!

BATTLE HYMN OF THE REPUBLIC
STRUMMED VERSION

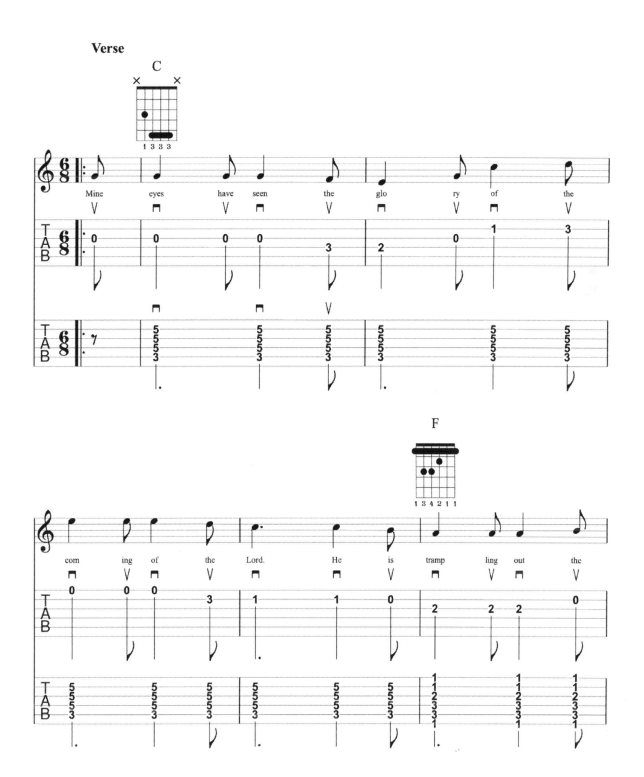

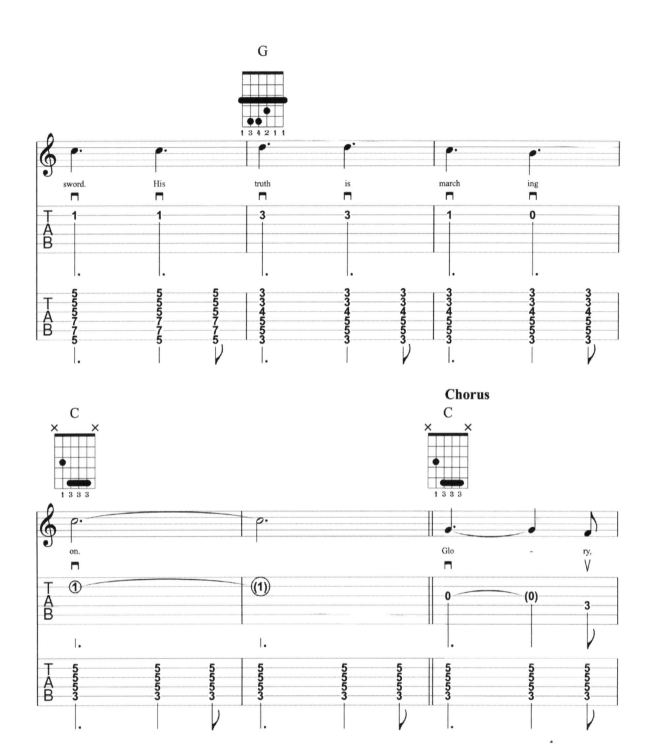

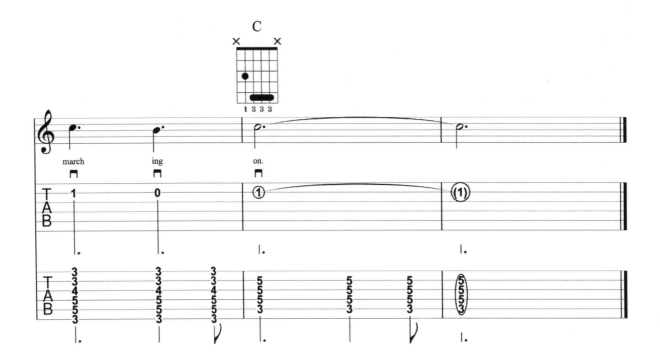

BATTLE HYMN OF THE REPUBLIC
FINGERPICKED VERSION

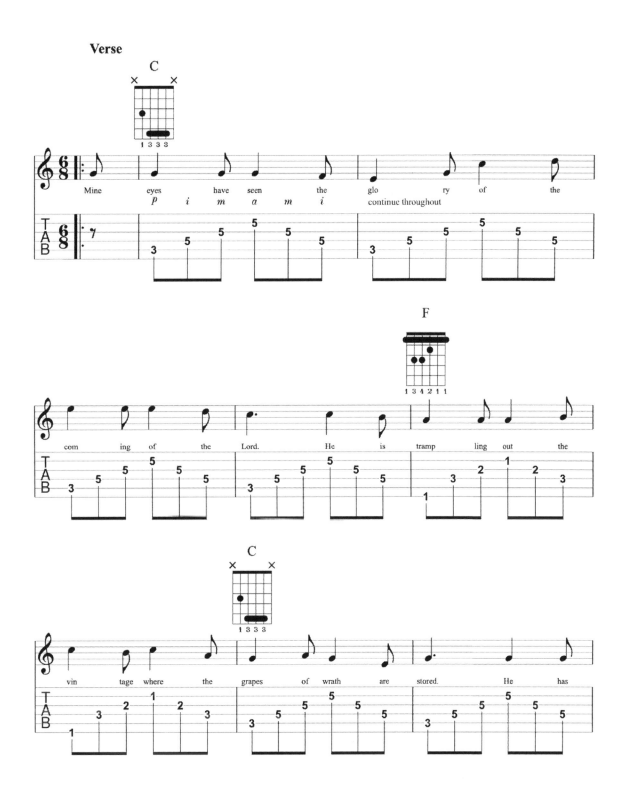

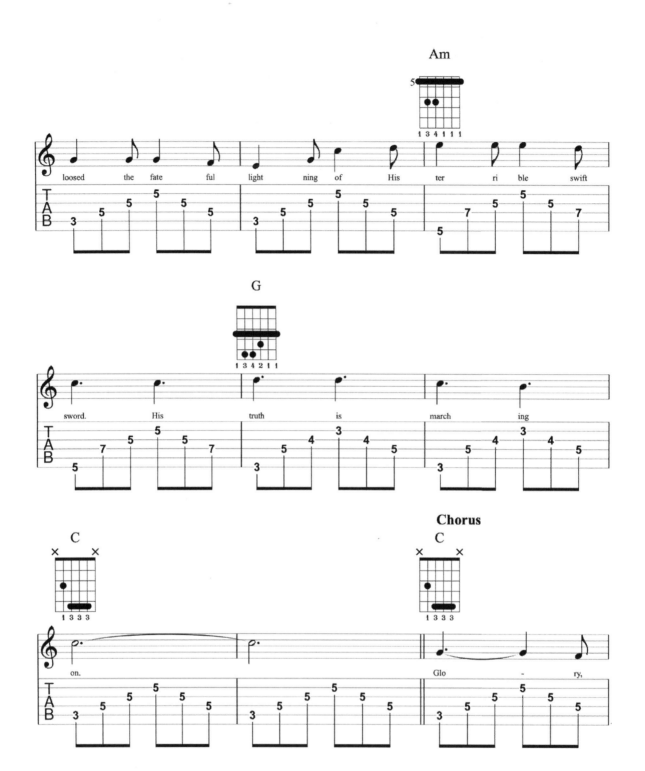

Chorus

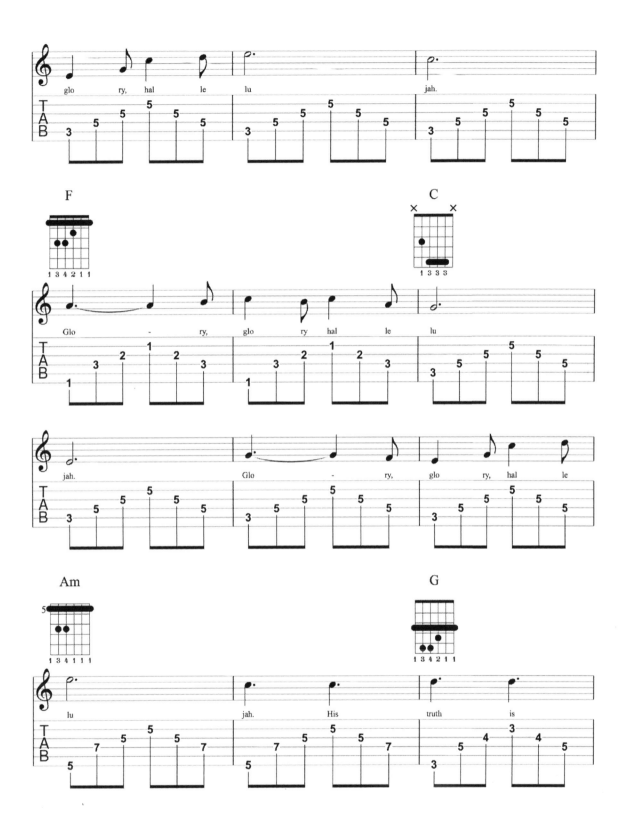

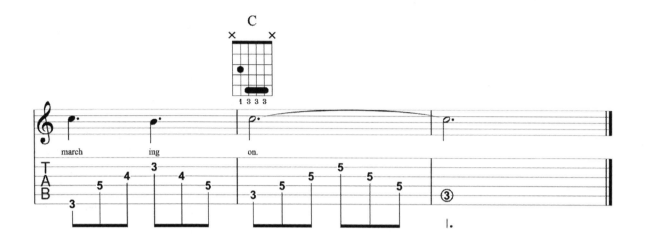

march   ing   on.

A FEW FINAL THOUGHTS

I hope this book has helped you achieve your goal of becoming an acoustic guitarist. The 100+ pages contain a lot of information and music, so hopefully you didn't feel overwhelmed while you worked your way through it. As I stated in the book's introduction, the material isn't going anywhere—you can always come back to it at a later time and work through it at your own pace. In fact, I encourage you to practice the material a second—or even third—time. At the very least, spend some time practicing the material that you struggled with when you went through the book the first time.

But the learning process doesn't end with this book. Now that you're equipped with dozens of chord voicings and chord types, strum patterns, picking patterns, and techniques, I encourage you to learn as many songs as you can, as this is truly the best way to learn the instrument and grow as a guitarist. A simple Google search will turn up guitar tabs and chord progressions to just about any song you can think of. If you're a visual learner, find tutorials on YouTube to learn songs or techniques that interest you.

Of course, I'm a firm believer in using books to further your guitar education, as well. I suggest finding one or two additional books that will help you become the guitarist you want to be. For example, if your goal is to become a better fingerstyle guitarist, then search out a good fingerstyle book on Amazon. Or, if you're really interested in classical guitar, several good books can be found on that very topic with a quick search. My own company, Troy Nelson Music, has published several books that might interest you:

12 Easy Classical Masterpieces for Solo Guitar
16 Easy Christmas Songs for Fingerpicking Guitar
Creative Songwriting on Guitar
Learn 14 Chord Progressions for Guitar in 14 Days
Master Music Theory for Guitar in 14 Days
Master Pentatonic Scales for Guitar in 14 Days
Memorize & Master the Guitar Fretboard in 14 Days

Whatever you choose as your next step, I hope you find much success in your guitar studies! Good luck!

70476017R00062